SHROPSHIRE

Remembering 1914–18

D0995886

JANET DOODY

The
History
Press

*This book has been produced to commemorate the
experiences and sacrifices made by the
people of Shropshire throughout the First World War.
The individuals whose names appear within these pages,
with their letters, photographs and reminisces,
represent all who fought in the war —
all those who produced armaments and foodstuffs,
all those who, in all forms, cared for others,
and of course all those who never returned.*

First published 2014

The History Press
The Mill, Brimscombe Port
Stroud, Gloucestershire, GL5 2QG
www.thehistorypress.co.uk

British Library Cataloguing in Publication Data.
A catalogue record for this book is available from the British Library.

ISBN 978 0 7509 5844 8

Typesetting and origination by The History Press
Printed in Great Britain

CONTENTS

TIMELINE

1914

28 June

*Assassination of Archduke
Franz Ferdinand in Sarajevo*

3 July

*King George V visits the Royal
Agricultural Show at Shrewsbury*

4 August

Great Britain declares war on Germany

23 August

Battle of Tannenberg commences

6 September

First Battle of the Marne

19 October

First Battle of Ypres

27 November

*Baschurch VAD Hospital receives
its first wounded servicemen*

1915

13 March

*Maurice Darby is killed in action
and his body is brought home*

25 April

Allied landing at Gallipoli

7 May

*Germans torpedo and
sink the Lusitania*

31 May

First German Zeppelin raid on London

2 October

*'Great Recruiting Rallies' are
held throughout Shropshire*

20 December

*Allies finish their evacuation of
and withdrawal from Gallipoli*

1916

24 January

The British Government introduces conscription

21 February

Battle of Verdun commences

31 May

Battle of Jutland

4 June

Brusilov Offensive commences

1 July

First day of the Battle of the Somme with 57,000 British casualties

8 July

Woodhouse Colliery Accident in which seven men nearly lost their lives

20 July

A huge fire occurs at Messrs James Cock & Co. of Shrewsbury

27 August

Italy declares war on Germany

18 December

Battle of Verdun ends

1917

7 March

Mrs Katherine Harley of Condover is killed in Serbia

6 April

The United States declares war on Germany

9 April

Battle of Arras

9 July

Private Denis J. Blakemore of Shrewsbury is executed for desertion

31 July

Third Battle of Ypres (Passchendaele)

20 August

Third Battle of Verdun

26 October

Second Battle of Passchendaele

20 November

Battle of Cambrai

7 December

USA declares war on Austria-Hungary

1918

3 March

*Russia and the Central Powers
sign the Treaty of Brest-Litovsk*

10 March

*Private Harold Whitfield is
awarded the Victoria Cross*

21 March

Second Battle of the Somme

6 June

*The Croix de Guerre avec Palme is
awarded to the 4th Battalion KSLI*

15 July

Second Battle of the Marne

8 August

*Battle of Amiens, first stage of
the Hundred Days Offensive*

22 September

The Great Allied Balkan victory

27 September

Storming of the Hindenburg Line

8 November

Armistice negotiations commence

9 November

*Kaiser Wilhelm II abdicates,
Germany is declared a Republic*

11 November

*Armistice Day, cessation of
hostilities on the Western Front*

1919

5 August

*Shropshire Peace Day and
Victory March in Shrewsbury*

ACKNOWLEDGEMENTS

With thanks to the Ironbridge Gorge Museum Trust, especially Joanne Smith in the library and archives, and to volunteers Jim Cooper and John Powell without whose assistance this book would not have been possible. Also to Ray Farlow and Brian Curran for access to their postcard collections.

INTRODUCTION

On 28 June 1914, Archduke Franz Ferdinand, heir to the Austrian-Hungarian throne, undertook a state visit to Sarajevo and was assassinated. During the following July, negotiations for a peace settlement took place throughout Europe, but as these began to break down so alliances were formed between the Western Powers. On 28 July 1914, Austria declared war on Serbia, which led to further declarations of war until, on 4 August 1914, the Central Powers of Germany and Austria were at war with the Allied Powers of Russia, Serbia, France, Belgium and Britain.

The events escalating throughout Europe went largely unnoticed by the British public; for Members of Parliament there were troubles at home in the form of industrial unrest and the violent campaigns of the suffrage movement. Of greatest concern was the Irish Home Rule Question – the demand for Home Rule by the Catholic Southern Irish and the refusal of the Protestant North to be governed from Dublin. An extract from the diary of King George V, on 30 July 1914, illustrates how late the government was to recognise the severity of the developments in Europe: 'The debate in the House of Commons on the Irish question today has been postponed on account of the gravity of the European situation.'

Shropshire

At the beginning of the twentieth century, the rural landscape of Shropshire, dominated by large country estates, was still much as it had been throughout Queen Victoria's reign. The landowners were prominent in the administration of the county and also, through the tenanted farms and cottages, in the life of much of the agricultural workforce.

In the industrial districts – where traditional extractive industries of mining and quarrying, together with iron and steelmaking, were conducted – the large companies had replaced the landed estate. Here the company directors became involved in the local administration and provided its workforce with company houses.

However, along with the rest of the country, Shropshire society was gradually changing as its industries struggled with economic decline. Agriculture suffered from the increasing importation of foodstuffs, particularly grain, whilst traditional manufacturing concerns faced competition from markets both home and abroad.

One of the most significant changes to the rural landscape during the post-war period was the sale of the large estates, whilst in urban areas a number of companies did not survive or significantly reduced their operations. Although the war years did see a recovery in prosperity, this is now recognised as a delay in what was a long-term recession.

1

OUTBREAK OF WAR

Shropshire's Heritage

Shropshire, England's largest inland county, covers over 1,300 square miles and is situated between the Welsh mountains and the Midlands. The River Severn roughly divides the county, with the sandstone plains to the north and east, and the uplands of hills and dales in the south and west. At the centre of this predominately rural county, surrounded by the River Severn, is Shrewsbury, the county town and seat of local government.

The contrasts in the landscape dictated the type of farming undertaken: the flat plains of the north-east supported dairy and arable farming, whilst the hill and moorland country of the south specialised in livestock, especially sheep. The majority of the land was worked by tenant farmers in countryside largely dominated by the country estate and included dwellings known as 'tied cottages' which housed the farm workers. Much of this workforce was dependent on the landowner for both employment and a home. For the vast majority the relationship was amicable but any disagreements could result in not only unemployment but also homelessness for the labourers' family.

The agricultural economy had been in steady decline since the 1870s, helped by the increasing importation of foodstuffs, especially cheap cereal crops from the United States. As unemployment amongst farmworkers increased, so too did adverts in the newspapers encouraging emigration abroad, especially

Map of Shropshire showing the topography of the county around the time of the First World War.

to Canada, and many from Shropshire took this opportunity. A growing number of arable farmers also began to change to the less labour intensive livestock farming, in particular dairy production.

The demand for milk increased as the urban areas of the West Midlands grew. Transporting large quantities over a distance, however, had yet to be developed and Shropshire produced far more than could be consumed within its boundaries. Although a quantity was sent to Birmingham, the majority was used in the developing cheese and chocolate industries.

The manufacture of cheese and butter as a local farm-based product to use excess milk had long been carried out by farmer's wives. They had sold it either directly from the farm gate or in the local markets; the popularity of specialist cheese fairs and markets, especially in the Whitchurch area, had grown considerably. Commercial creameries had begun to move into rural centres: at Minsterley, a creamery was established by 1906 and had started to supply milk to Birmingham. Almost as a by-product in times when surplus milk was available, these creameries started to make cheese and, by 1915, one quarter of all Cheshire cheese was produced in Shropshire.

As the British public's appetite for chocolate increased, companies such as Cadbury's at Bournville looked to expand. In 1911, Cadbury's opened a factory at Knighton, just over the Staffordshire border, and became the largest purchaser of Shropshire's liquid milk.

The north-west uplands around Oswestry had hill country similar to the south-west, where sheep farming dominated but there was also a small concentration of mining and quarrying activity. The Clee Hills in South Shropshire had been mined for generations, but by the end of the nineteenth century it was the basalt or 'Dhu Stone' that the Abdon Clee Stone Quarrying Company needed for building and road construction.

The industries outside the major coalfield area were, in general, reliant on farming for business – producing and supplying animal feedstuffs, fertilizers and seed, whilst the iron foundries manufactured agricultural implements and equipment. On the coalfield itself, the long-established names in the traditional heavy industries were still the major employers but were struggling as competition in other areas grew. The Madeley Wood Company operated a number of collieries mining coal, ironstone and clay and the Coalbrookdale Company continued to produce and develop kitchen ranges as well as the more mundane pots and pans. In addition to these larger companies, there were also a number of individually owned brick and roofing tile manufacturers.

New markets had begun to open both at home and abroad as improvements in urban living were implemented. The Coalbrookdale Company took advantage of developments in house building to produce cast-iron drain pipes and guttering, whilst the brick and roofing tile concerns – using the local clays – specialised in 'Broseley' roofing tiles. The Coalport China Company attended the World's Fair in 1893 in Chicago, followed by a visit from the Duchess of York (later Queen Mary), which boosted sales for a while. The Craven Dunnill and Maw companies were producing encaustic and ceramic tiles that could be found in the London underground stations, in new hotels, hospitals and even palaces, throughout the world.

Probably the most successful business in the area at the time, with a workforce approaching 4,000, was the Lilleshall Company. This was a large conglomerate incorporating mining, iron and steel making and finishing, light and heavy engineering and the manufacture of clay products. They had developed close working relationships with a number of German engineering companies, especially in the manufacture of large gas engines. In 1912, in partnership with two other German concerns, coking ovens, a crushing and screening plant and an asphalt plant were constructed.

The Lilleshall Company, like other industrial concerns, became actively involved in the lives of their employees; they helped to provide social and religious facilities, and a hospital as well as housing. The rents were deducted from wages and, once the tenant left the company's employment, the house too would have to be vacated in a similar way to the tied agricultural cottages on the country estate.

In 1913 the Lilleshall Company won a contract to install the sewage works in Bombay, India. Richard Frith and Reece Barker (pictured here) were among the workmen and engineers who oversaw the installation. (Ironbridge Gorge Museum Trust)

The Boards of Directors for these industrial concerns could be viewed as the urban equivalent of the rural landowner – involved in the county council administration, standing as councillors, serving on various county committees and as local magistrates and Justices of the Peace.

1914

At the beginning of 1914 the daily life for most working people still revolved around the agricultural calendar of sowing, haymaking, harvest and ploughing; even in the urban areas the countryside was never far away. Most industrial workers had access to a garden or allotment to grow food for the home; some kept poultry or even a pig, with rabbit, fish or game occasional welcome additions, however obtained.

Although numbers attending church and chapel were not as high as they had once been, for many people it was still the focus of social engagement, with fetes, concerts and parades known as demonstrations. The churches were also involved in the organisation of outings to local beauty spots and Charles Peskin,

St Peters church, Priorslee, the boys' 1914 football team. How many of these boys went to war and how many returned? (Kindly loaned by Jim Cooper)

15

BICTON FLOWER SHOW

ON BANK HOLIDAY, MONDAY, AUGUST 3rd.

OPEN CLASSES for FRUIT, FLOWERS, and VEGETABLES.

TENDERS are invited from Amusement Caterers, Roundabouts, SideShows, etc.; also Band of 12 performers, to be sent in at once.

Particulars from Phillips and Richards, Secretaries, Marblewood, Bicton Heath.

WELLINGTON COLLEGE GROUNDS.

FRIDAY, AUGUST 14th, 1914.

Under the auspices of the Wellington and District Scouts Association,

A GARDEN PARTY

WILL be held in the above grounds (by kind permission of Mr J. Bayey), in aid of the Boy Scout Local Troop Funds.

For further particulars see bills and later announcements.

A. B. HARPER, Hon. Sec.

PUBLIC NOTICE.

ST. GEORGE'S AND OAKENGATES

ATHLETIC CLUB SPORTS

Will this year again be held on the

OLD WAKES TUESDAY, SEPTEMBER 1st, 1914,

On the SPORTS' GROUND, ST. GEORGE'S. (under A.A.A. and N.C.U. Rules),

when the usual VALUABLE PRIZES will be offered

Notices and adverts of some of the events proposing to take place throughout Shropshire during the late summer of 1914.

from Ironbridge, describes a typical outing in his diary for 16 July 1914: 'Ironbridge Church Choir Trip to Liverpool and New Brighton, fares 4/10 [4s 10d – about 24p]. Dinner at the Edinburgh Café in Paradise Street, 1/9 [1s 9d].'

Sport of all kinds became increasingly popular, either for taking part or spectating. Most communities had a least one football team and there were also cricket, billiards and bowls teams, all with organised leagues and fixtures. The local county newspapers carried a complete page of sports reports and results every week.

One of the main features throughout the year was that of the agricultural and horticulture shows, which came in many guises: from the small village flower or vegetable show to the huge county agricultural events. These shows included many classes which provided competition for town and country workers alike; such classes were not restricted to horticulture, moreover, but included small livestock such as poultry or rabbits as well. In Broseley, the annual Potato Show held at the New Inn was very competitive and always well supported.

The Royal Agricultural Show

Whilst significant changes were taking place in the east of Europe during the summer of 1914, in Shropshire the month of July brought great excitement with probably little thought of possible war: Shrewsbury had been selected by the Royal Agricultural Society of England to host their annual show. This was to be held over five days – from Tuesday, 30 June to

THE ROYAL SHOW
AT SHREWSBURY.
COUNTY TOWN JUSTIFIES ITS SELECTION.
SUCCESS AT ALL POINTS.
LOYAL WELCOME TO THE KING.
HUGE CROWDS OF CHEERING PEOPLE.

Headlines in the Shrewsbury Chronicle in August 1914.

Saturday, 4 July – on the racecourse at Monkmoor in Shrewsbury and, on Friday, 3 July, His Majesty King George V was to visit.

The *Shrewsbury Chronicle* reported that (on Friday):

Visitors began to arrive at an early hour. They came not singly as spies but in battalions by rail and road. The hoot of the motor horn was seldom silent, the tinkling of the cyclists' bell was continuous. Every garage was fully utilized. The stables at all hostelries had not a stall which was not tenanted by a horse. The yards congested with vehicles.

On the day of the king's visit it was estimated that by 5.00 p.m. there had been over 38,500 visitors. The royal train steamed into Shrewsbury station at 12.45 p.m. to be greeted by all the local dignitaries and a platform decorated in the borough colours of blue and gold.

Many companies, including the Coalbrookdale Ironworks, closed for the day to allow their workforce the opportunity to see the king. Charles Peskin and a group of friends from Coalbrookdale took the opportunity and went on 'the 2nd crowded train from Ironbridge. fare 1/6 [1*s* 6*d* – about 7½p]'. The train stopped before Shrewsbury station for so long that the group left it and walked into town joining the crowds on Wyle Cop:

POPULATION OF SHROPSHIRE

The total population of Shropshire, taken from the 1911 census, was 246,307. This was made up of 121,835 males and 124,472 females.

The number of men aged between 19 and 38 years, and eligible for enlistment (overseas), was over 33,000 and of these about 18,000 were unmarried.

Reserve Ambulance, nurses, Regulars. Scouts, Boys Brigade [were] lining street [with a] guard of honour at the corner of the Square, [and] High Street. The King's carriage stopped immediately in front of us within talking distance. Wet in the morning and went beautiful after 11.30.

Throughout July the local press covered little of the developments taking place over Europe; instead the weekly newspapers concentrated on the Agricultural Show. They reported in detail the spectacle of the show and devoted pages to publishing the results of all the show classes.

The summer weather of 1914 was glorious, and the holidays were uppermost in the minds of most people, probably throughout Britain. During Easter the railway traffic to Wellington was reported as heavy, with a large number of holidaymakers visiting the Wrekin where 'conditions for a good climb were all that could be desired'. The Cottage on the Wrekin, later known as the 'Half-Way House', provided refreshments for walkers, being a convenient resting place to partake of an ice cream. It also had a dining room for about fifty people that was renowned for its 'duck dinners'.

The royal visit to the Agricultural Show. (Kindly loaned by Ray Farlow)

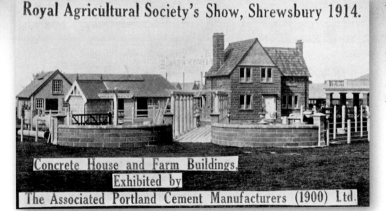

Royal Agricultural Society's Show, Shrewsbury 1914.

Concrete House and Farm Buildings
Exhibited by
The Associated Portland Cement Manufacturers (1900) Ltd.

A postcard of the Associated Portland Cement Manufacturers Display and Exhibition at the Agricultural Show in 1914. (Kindly loaned by Brian Curran)

However, not all families were able to enjoy their holiday, as one schoolgirl at the time remembered:

> We set off for our usual seaside visit – for a fortnight we thought. The next day came the shocking news that Britain was at war. My father immediately sent us to pack up all our things ready to return to Shrewsbury, in case the passenger trains were withdrawn to leave the lines clear for the movement of troops.

Declaration of War

From Saturday, 8 August 1914, the local newspapers realised the events taking place in Europe could no longer be ignored:

> EUROPE ABLAZE – GERMANY AND AUSTRIA AT WAR WITH GREAT BRITAIN, FRANCE, RUSSIA, SERVIA [*sic*] BELGIUM, HOLLAND AND MONTENEGRO.

> All efforts to secure peace between the great European Powers have failed and war is raging throughout Europe. Never has there been a war of such monstrous size, as the number of combatants so far involved totals more than twenty millions. Great Britain has at last herself been drawn into the struggle.

The previous week's events were then reported day by day culminating with:

TUESDAY – GREAT BRITAIN DECLARES WAR

His Majesty's Government have declared to the German Government that a state of war exists between Great Britain and Germany as from 11.00pm on August 4th

The mobilisation of the British Army began immediately, with the Reservists and Territorial Forces quickly following. The county's regular regiment was the King's Shropshire Light Infantry (KSLI), together with the volunteers of the Territorials, Shropshire Yeomanry and the Royal Shropshire Horse Artillery. The regular soldiers of the 1st and 2nd Battalions KSLI were soon on their way to France, followed by the 4th Battalion (Territorials), who left Shrewsbury on 5 August for Barry, near Cardiff. The mounted volunteer units were then 'embodied' or called up which, in most cases, was achieved very quickly. The Shropshire Yeomanry

THE WAR.

Your Country Needs YOU.

A movement is being organised to raise one or more Companies of Infantry consisting of Professional and Business men, to complete the New Battalion of the

KING'S SHROPSHIRE LIGHT INFANTRY

I appeal with the utmost confidence to all Salopians to take advantage of this opportunity to present themselves for enlistment at the **MUSIC HALL, SHREWSBURY,** on **MONDAY EVENING NEXT,** the 7th inst., at 8 o'clock.

EDWARD CURETON,

Guildhall, Shrewsbury,   Deputy Mayor.
September 2nd, 1914.

God Save the King.

Kings Shropshire Light Infantry recruitment advert placed in the local newspapers.

received their call-up letters the day after war was declared, which saw 'C' Squadron leaving Ludlow just three days later.

Crowds gathered with great excitement in every town to watch the men leave, cheering and waving them on their way. In Oswestry, the mayor, Alderman Charles Williams, wore his chain of office and addressed the Territorials at the Great Western Railway Station, 'wishing them God speed' before they left on the train. Schoolchildren remember seeing soldiers marching past singing 'It's a Long Way to Tipperary' full of optimism and enthusiasm to do their duty.

SHROPSHIRE TOURISTS STRANDED
The declaration of war left a number of British tourists stranded on the Continent. Miss Ellis, a schoolteacher from Mount Oswald, Oswestry, cabled worried friends to say she was safe in Switzerland, together with two more ladies on a Cook's excursion.

Wellington Journal and Shrewsbury News

Enlistment

However, as Britain's standing army was small in number, it soon became clear that many more men were needed. There was, for the moment, no question of conscription; instead Lord Kitchener's now-famous poster called for volunteers and many rushed to enlist. In Shropshire, recruitment centres were set up in all the local towns where queues of men stood waiting to sign on. The Shropshire Yeomanry, a mounted division, reported that it was 'not difficult obtaining recruits' – though a number were rejected as they could not ride!

The local newspapers enthusiastically carried accounts of enlistments, especially where brothers were involved, and the report always included the encouragement and support given by their mother as well as details of the number of family members now fighting for their country: 'A record number of brothers from one family now serving in the Army has been established in Shropshire.'

Mrs Price from Gretton, near Craven Arms, who had been married twice, had *seventeen* sons serving in the army: Joe and Fred were serving with the Welsh Fusiliers; Richard and William

The youngest sons of Mr and Mrs Cox (of Monkhopton, near Bridgnorth) were all in the Regular Army.
Clockwise from top left, Richard Cox, age 23, served in the Grenadier Guards; Mr Cox (father); Charlie,
age 21, served in the Army Service Corps; Tom, age 28, also in the Army Service Corps; Edward,
age 25, served with the KSLI; and George, age 30, served as a sergeant in the Coldstream Guards.
(Wellington Journal and Shrewsbury News, *5 December 1914)*

enlisted in Lord Kitchener's Army at the outbreak of the war; whilst Ernest, Alfred, Harry, Albert, George, Charles, Thomas, Frank, Eddie, Walter and Cyril were serving with the Shropshire Regiment. The latest recruit, John Davies, aged 29, had gone from Craven Arms to Wellington to enlist. He said he 'felt he could not stay behind when all his brothers and step-brothers were serving their King and country'. The report went on to state that 'Davies is a typical farm hand and looks like being able to stand the hard work he will be called to do in a long and arduous campaign'.

One young man, W. Newill, employed as a core maker at Coalbrookdale, said: 'I tried to enlist in Shrewsbury in the county regiment but owing to my trade they wouldn't take me so we went to Birmingham … an officer asked for volunteers I popped forward – I had had enough of this messing around – and chose the Grenadier Guards.'

The age of these new recruits was not always rigorously checked: one young man from Ketley, Harry Jeffs (the son of John and Florence Jeffs), had been born on 26 September 1899. He enlisted on 1 July 1915, stating his age to be 19 years and 5 months, and served in the 3rd and 7th KSLI as Private 16152. He was sent out to France on 9 February 1916. After developing trench foot during March of that year, he was hospitalised and it seems his true age was soon discovered. He was discharged on 29 April 1916 but re-enlisted on 7 October 1916 although still only 17 years of age. Despite stating a preference for the Royal Flying Corps, Jeffs was assigned to the Royal Field Artillery and was again sent to France in March 1917. Sadly Private Jeffs was killed on 7 May that same year.

In rural areas young men walked for miles in order to enlist and it appeared to the children that they 'all seemed to go in one day leaving the village silent'. Recruits poured in so quickly in those first few weeks that the large numbers were difficult to administer; eventually many were signed up but sent home again to be called back at a later date. Len Edwards from Ironbridge recalled he initially enlisted in Ironbridge for the Royal Horse Artillery at Woolwich; he then waited and finally went to Shrewsbury and enlisted at Coleham in the Shropshire Yeomanry.

Private
Bert Oakes

Private 22219 Bertram 'Bert' Watson Oakes of the 9th Battalion Kings Shropshire Light Infantry was sent to 28 Hut 4th Camp, Prees Heath in March 1916 for training. He recorded his experiences in letters to his parents in Broseley and writes here about the food he received:

I've just had my dinner, viz. beef, potatoes & peas, stewed rhubarb & milk, not bad, & we have pineapples, margarine & bread for tea, this is to make up for bully beef & biscuits yesterday I suppose, we couldn't eat the latter, they were too hard, just like dog biscuits.

He also described the training they were required to undertake:

I will just give you an illustration of a day's work. Six o'clock got out of bed, dress, make bed & tidy room, first parade 6.30 am. Physical training till 7.45 am, breakfast, buttons cleaned, shaving & boots till 8.45 am. Bayonet fighting till 10 o'clock. Marching & other drill till 12 pm, rest & dinner till 1.45 pm, Musketry till 4.00 pm, the trenching digging comes in the drill from 11 till 12. Then some nights we have an hour lecture & others silent marching to the trenches in the dark. We get dreadfully dirty digging & carrying turfs to cover the parapets of the trenches with. It's like being rabbits, for its all underground work, digging one's self in & then lying in it wet or dry.

We've been on a bombing course this week and the exam is on Monday but this child does not want to pass as a bomber it's too dangerous, I'd rather have my rifle & bayonet than little balls of iron, they explode in 5 seconds & that doesn't leave long to throw. Then I shall try & get in the Signalling Corps.

A letter from Bert Oakes to his parents, 1916. The headed notepaper is the 'Wesleyan Soldiers' Institute' at Prees Heath and Bert says he has seen Percy Instone who was also from Broseley; Percy 'was pleased to have someone he knows', for many young men this was their first time away from home and many would have felt lonely and homesick. (Author's collection)

A rare image of Bert Oakes with his wife Gertie. They married in 1916, just before Bert left for France. Sadly they were to have only a sort time together as Bert was killed on 30 September 1917. (Toby Neal, Shropshire Star)

Prees Heath Camp, the Town Hut, YMCA 3, Will (regiment and surname unknown) wrote to 'Little Margery' in Kentish Town, London saying, 'This is the Y.M.C.A. Hut I go sometimes in the evenings. I had quite forgot that it was your birthday last Wednesday, and I will wish you many happy returns of the day. Thank you very much for the mittens they keep my hands nice and warm with love from Will.' (Kindly loaned by Ray Farlow)

Advertisement in Kelly's Trade Directory for Walter Harper, 'Artistic Portraiture' dated 1917. A large number of soldiers in their new uniforms would have visited similar establishments to this for a photograph before they left to go overseas. The agricultural nature of the area and probably the majority of Harper's business is reflected in 'animal photography a speciality'; many farmers would have photographs of their prize-winning stock.

Those who were accepted and drafted into a regiment then needed to be equipped and sent for training, but the demand for uniforms and equipment exceeded supply. A report to the Shropshire County Council stated that it was difficult to equip the new recruits; they were forced to parade for weeks in emergency blue uniforms or even 'mufti' (civilian clothes) and 'every description of hat was on view, from bowlers to straw boaters'. The 7th Battalion reported that 'old red coats' were on parade, with poles, stakes and even pit props in place of rifles, but the keenness and enthusiasm of the men made up for the lack of rifles and uniforms.

It was not only the infantry that had problems in the supply of equipment: whilst the Shropshire Yeomanry was stationed for training at Brogyntyn Park, near Oswestry, the ladies of the town (under the leadership of Lady Harlech) made straw mattresses for the whole regiment in one day at the cost of £18.

As men continued to enlist, new battalions were formed with the sole purpose of training and organising their onward posting to the Regular Army. The 3rd (Special Reserve) Battalion KSLI left Shrewsbury on 9 August 1914 to be stationed at Pembroke Dock where, by 15 September 1914, they had sent their first 100 men to France. The 9th (Reserve) Service Battalion KSLI was formed in the autumn of 1914; it too trained recruits and organised their transfer to the regiments. Initially based in Pembroke Dock, it was then returned to Shropshire in 1915 and stationed at Prees Heath where it remained until 1918 when the battalion was disbanded.

Military Camps

In order to meet the ever-increasing demand for trained
soldiers, purpose-built military camps began to be constructed.
Prees Heath, situated 3 miles south of Whitchurch, was an area of
wild heath and grassland that was deemed eminently suitable for
such a camp. It was described in the local newspapers as a 'wooden
town' and consisted of around 900 huts for the accommodation
and training of (initially) over 18,000 soldiers. The buildings also
included officers' quarters and a drill yard, together with riding
schools and stabling for horses as well as shops and a cinema;
electricity was brought to the camp before it was established in the
nearby town of Whitchurch. Roads were constructed, tramways
laid and a railway siding was built to connect it with the London
and North Western Railway. Many regiments were sent to Prees
Heath for training, including the Highland Light Infantry, so the
final number of soldiers to pass through the camp were said to be
between 25,000 and 30,000.

At the outbreak of the war, Major Wynne Corrie, owner of
Park Hall (which stood 1 mile east of Oswestry), offered his
home for the war effort. It was taken over by the army and a

*Prees Heath Camp –
the reverse of this
card states 'the sidings
down the Ash Road',
and shows the delivery
of materials by rail
in order to construct
the 'wooden town'.
(Kindly loaned by
Ray Farlow)*

Prees Heath Camp showing row upon row of wooden huts or barracks along the Prees Road. (Kindly loaned by Ray Farlow)

William Prince with a comrade at a training camp before going out to France. (Ironbridge Gorge Museum Trust)

camp was constructed in the grounds. Opened in the spring of 1915 the site was in constant use throughout the war, housing over 20,000 troops.

However, in the excitement of preparing to go to war, many of the young recruits forgot the routine and discipline involved in being a soldier. One night, on returning to camp on their motorcycle, Corporal Deakin and Trooper Inions of the Shropshire Yeomanry failed to stop when challenged by the sentry. The guard opened fire over their heads and in the ensuing melee the horses stampeded and it was some time before order was restored!

Remount Centres

The army established a number of remount centres throughout the country in order to find, train and distribute animals for war work. Shropshire had gained a national reputation in the breeding of good horses, with dealers coming from all over the country to buy at the local horse sales. The local stud farms and breeders employed grooms who were experienced in handling and caring for horses and consequently the army set up a number of remount centres within the county.

Leighton Hall Remount Depot, Leighton
Leighton Hall, situated in the village of Leighton on the north side of the River Severn between Atcham and Ironbridge, was the residence of Thomas Kynnersley, deputy lieutenant and Justice of the Peace. The meadows adjacent to the river were used for grazing, making it an ideal location for a remount depot. Initially suitable horses were commandeered from local farmers, but as more and more animals were needed they began to be brought in from abroad, especially from Canada. Horses were also redistributed from other regiments where they were no longer needed; it was reported that the Shropshire Yeomanry troopers, on becoming an infantry regiment, were 'very sad' when the remount officers took their horses away.

The original stable yard of Leighton Hall with animals fully trained and ready to go to France. The first three vehicles are drawn by horses and have ridden 'drivers' so are probably ready for gun carriage, whilst the far vehicle is pulled by mules which suggested these have been trained for general haulage work. (Ironbridge Gorge Museum Trust)

Once the animals were in training they were generally kept under cover and, to accommodate them, the stabling at Leighton was greatly expanded. A number of quality horses were used as riding animals by officers and these were housed in Leighton Hall's original brick-built stables and loose boxes. The majority of the horses, however, were intended either for general haulage or for gun carriage work and these were accommodated in specially erected large 'Dutch' barns, in which crude stalls were constructed. In addition to the horses, a large number of mules were also kept but these, it seems, were turned out in yards with field shelters.

Animals were also boarded out locally. Jack Oakley, whose family ran a haulage concern in Broseley, recalls having as many as 120 army horses to look after. They were given 25s per week per horse and the animals were stabled throughout the town. Many of the horses were 'not good', although whether this referred to them being not of good quality or of being difficult to train is uncertain.

A large number of grooms were employed in this work and, as men enlisted, they needed to be replaced. Adverts in the national press called for men with experience on farms and in hunting yards, or 'any men with an understanding of horses', for which good wages would be given. The grooms at Leighton Hall slept in dormitories, with meals provided in a communal dining room all housed in the original stable buildings.

The grooms' dormitory at the Leighton Remount Centre. Two of the grooms are seated and the couple standing by the door are probably the housekeepers. (Ironbridge Gorge Museum Trust)

The training of the waggon and gun carriage horses and mules seems to have taken place within the stable yard using up to six grooms. Many of these animals arrived almost semi-wild and certainly very frightened so it could be dangerous work; in 1915 Joseph Robert Launchbury, an experienced stud groom at Leighton, was killed after being kicked by one of the horses.

CONSIDERABLE EXCITEMENT
'Considerable excitement has been manifest in Oakengates and St Georges, where a number of Germans employed locally have obeyed the call to their Fatherland and left the district on Monday and Tuesday.'

Wellington Journal and Shrewsbury News

Underdale Hall, Shrewsbury

A very different remount centre was located at Underdale Hall in Shrewsbury, where a rather eccentric Lieutenant Mike Rimmington was in charge. He had been wounded in France and, after recovering, had been appointed to the Army Remount Department. At Underdale, animals that had been classed as 'unmanageable horses and savage mules condemned to death

An extremely well-turned-out soldier of the Shropshire Yeomanry together with his horse. (Ironbridge Gorge Museum Trust)

by the authorities' were retrained. Lieutenant Rimmington was able to use his remarkable skill with horses, adopting a policy of using neither whip nor spur but understanding and kindness. It was said that he kept a 'killer' horse called Crippin and used to walk amongst his other horses firing blanks from a revolver to get them used to the noises on the war front!

He also, unusually for the time, engaged three female grooms as assistants and together they gained the confidence of the animals so that, according to reports, he had not 'had one failure'. In 1917 he married Miss Woodforde, 'an expert horse woman' and one of those grooms whom he had originally appointed.

RECRUITING AID COMMITTEE REPORT
The committee relayed a report to Shropshire County Council on 20 April 1915 revealing that, from mobilisation to 31 December 1914, 4,628 men had enlisted: in January 1915 – 688 men, February – 334 men and March – 318 men. This, calculated the committee, meant that one in every five men had volunteered.

2

PREPARATIONS AT HOME

Shrewsbury was classed as one of the most important military centres in Britain and became a recruiting base for a number of regiments, not just county-affiliated ones. During peacetime the main barracks at Copthorne had been able to accommodate just over 240 men, by September 1914 up to 1,500 men were sleeping there and alterations had to be quickly carried out. Men and horses continued to pour into Shrewsbury so that public houses and hotels in the town also had to be commandeered, although these too were quickly filled. Soon soldiers were forced to sleep out in the street with such frequency that a large body of workmen were employed to convert the space under the old Market Hall in Shrewsbury into temporary lavatories.

The 16th Kings at Prees Heath Camp. The message on the reverse of this card says, 'Dear Nancy, just a few lines to let you know that I am leaving this camp tomorrow for Pembroke Dock, leaving Whitchuch at 9.o'clock morning. I would like to see you at Shrewsbury station to say goodbye. I have failed to have a pass, your affectionate Jack.' (Kindly loaned by Ray Farlow)

This arrangement, although enjoyable for those lucky enough to be in one of the hostelries, proved very unsatisfactory. This was especially problematic for the authorities since, with both men and equipment scattered throughout the town, basic training and even a simple roll call proved very difficult to implement. However, once the 3rd and later the 9th Service Battalions were established and stationed at their training bases, the system of enlisting new recruits ran relatively smoothly.

The 3rd (Special Reserve) Battalion saw no active service during the war, but served to train and supply reinforcements for the Regular Army. They had left Shrewsbury on 9 August 1914 and were, for much of the war, stationed at Bush Camp, Pembroke Dock, where they trained over 540 officers and 16,100 men for overseas. The 9th (Reserve) Service Battalion, formed on 1 November 1914, was also initially based at Pembroke Dock but later transferred to Prees Heath. Such was the connection between the regiment and this area of South Wales that, following the end of the conflict, a carved screen was erected to the men of the KSLI in the Lady Chapel of St John's church at Pembroke Dock. This memorial, together with a further eight oak panels, commemorated all those who had trained at Bush Camp and named those who had been killed in action.

At the outbreak of the war a separate military unit known as the Depot was created at Copthorne Barracks; basically an administrative centre, it was 'a hive of industry'. The duties of the Depot staff included providing supplies and equipment for units based in Shropshire as well as posting men to battalions, especially those discharged from hospitals. The chief task though, at least until February 1917 when it was taken over by the Ministry of National Service, was recruitment and by that date over 31,000 men had enlisted from Shropshire and the neighbouring counties of Herefordshire and Radnorshire.

Recruiting

The initial 'patriotic fervour' that drove volunteers to join the colours during the first months of the war had, towards Christmas 1914, begun to wane. Recruitment meetings and open-air rallies continued to take place throughout the county, but enlistment numbers were falling. In May 1915 the upper age limit for enlistment was increased from 38 to 40 years; however, there was competition for men not only on the fighting front but also at home in munitions and agricultural work. A shortage of skilled farm workers led to an instruction from the Shropshire County Office that 'certain classes of agricultural labourers should not be induced to enlist'.

A National Registration Act was introduced in July 1915 in an attempt to stimulate recruiting and also to discover how many men of military age were in work and how many of those were in 'starred' employment (that is, in jobs which were protected or highly skilled). This prompted discontent amongst the public who felt that this was to make way for conscription; however, Prime Minister Asquith assured Parliament that is 'not in the contempla-tion of the Government'. Towards the end of 1915, Lord Derby introduced a voluntary recruitment policy which became known as the Derby Scheme. The concept was that men who voluntarily registered would be called up only when necessary and married men only when the supply of single men was exhausted.

WELLINGTON JOURNAL AND SHREWSBURY NEWS. SEPTEMBER 25

G. R.

A Great Recruiting Rally

Will be held throughout **SHROPSHIRE**

ON SATURDAY, OCT. 2nd,

at the following centres :—

SHREWSBURY	DRAYTON	WEM	OSWESTRY
ELLESMERE	NEWPORT	BRIDGNORTH	SHIFNAL
WHITCHURCH	WELLINGTON	LUDLOW	DAWLEY DISTRICT

The Bands of the 2nd, 3rd, 3/4th King's Shropshire Light Infantry, and of the 3 4th Cheshires will Play in different centres

DO NOT WAIT !

If you are between the ages of 19 and 40, and over 5ft. 2in. in height.

JOIN THE KING'S SHROPSHIRE LIGHT INFANTRY.

All Infantry Regiments are now open.   Men are Urgently Needed.

GOD SAVE THE KING !

Notice of the 'Great Recruiting Rally' taking place throughout Shropshire. (Wellington Journal and Shrewsbury News, September 1915)

On 2 October a 'Great Recruiting Rally' was held throughout Shropshire encouraging voluntary enlistment, the results, though, were disappointing. In Oakengates the rally was held on Owens Field and the wet weather was said to have kept people away; but in Shifnal the meeting was held in the Town Hall and was regarded as a 'recruiting fiasco' which ended in failure, having speakers but no audience. The reports nevertheless went on to say the towns had 'nothing to be ashamed of', all had 'Done their Bit', with large numbers having already enlisted whilst others were engaged in munitions work.

Eventually, after much debate, conscription was introduced in the spring of 1916.

Volunteer Corps

Volunteer and Reserve units during the First World War were a complicated mixture. The National Reserve was made up of former soldiers who were too old or unfit for active service, they were called upon for guard duties at prisoner-of-war camps and government-controlled industrial premises. A number of Shropshire 'old soldiers' were involved in guarding the Brunner Mond Chemical Works in Cheshire, whilst members of No. 3 Company National Reserve KSLI were stationed at Handforth, a prisoner-of-war camp.

Civilians who, for any number of reasons, were not accepted for active military service began to come forward wanting to 'do their bit'. Oakengates and St Georges was probably typical of the local volunteer corps, made up of men too old or too young to fight in the regular services, those who were medically unfit and those who were employed in vital war work. Local doctors also helped out and Dr McCarthy acted as medical officer to the Lilleshall Company as well as attending industrial accidents never hesitating when he was called to go down the pits themselves.

Towns and villages throughout the county organised units along military lines, such as the Shrewsbury Athletes' Volunteer Corps and the Wellington Civilian Corps. These groups adopted a number of duties, such as helping to transport the wounded to hospital, assisting in recruiting and general Home Guard tasks. Initially the War Office did not officially recognise these

Comic postcard of a new recruit at a training camp. (Ironbridge Gorge Museum Trust)

IM HAVING A 'ELL OF A TIME.

citizen-based units but, as the local *Journal* reported, the military authorities gradually abandoned their 'somewhat hostile attitude towards' the volunteer movement and 'grudgingly consented' to acknowledge them.

Eventually units like the Shropshire Volunteer Training Corps based in Shrewsbury, a mixture of both uniformed and civilian staff which included women and Boy Scouts, were used in an administrative capacity attached to the battalions.

The Boy Scout troops quickly organised themselves. The 2nd Wellington, Oakengates and Shifnal troops mustered fifty-seven boys in six hours in preparation for active service. Their work in the main consisted of messenger duties and they earned the nickname of 'Dugdale's Dispatch Riders' after Mr Dugdale, the district commissioner. These duties were then extended to include the guarding of railway bridges and the guarding and checking of telegraph and telephone lines, which could involve up to 18.5 miles of wires. The boys on this work were paid 1*s* a day and earned a specially designed badge.

Oakengates and St Georges Volunteer Corps:

Back row standing*: George Mawdesley, W. Dallow, A. Allberry, F. Pendlebury, Mr Wylde, Albert Ball, R.L. Corbett, Mr Gee, Ernest Tranter, Ben Nicholls, W. Parker, Harry Davies, Tom Tranter and Jim Lee.*

Middle row seated *(some names only): 'Flash' Sneyd, J. Leeke, Arthur Tonks, Mr Meerson, Dr McCarthy (centre with long white stick), Lieutenant Smith, Price Jones, Tom Jones Sam Evans, Tom Ferriday and Mr Morgan.*

Front row*: Unknown, Mr Sneyd, Sergeant George Ward, Corporal D. Martin, Lance Corporal Tom Tagg.*

(Image kindly loaned by Jim Cooper)

Secondary and private schools encouraged their pupils to form cadet units. By July 1915, the headmaster of Adams Free Grammar School in Newport had set up a School Cadet Corp which became the 8th Company of the Secondary Schools Cadet Battalion attached to the 4th Battalion KSLI, with senior and junior platoons.

Shropshire Airfields

An expanding Royal Flying Corps, together with a need for safer airfields away from possible bombing raids, led army engineers to Shropshire and three airfields were eventually established at Monkmoor, Tern Hill and Shawbury.

Monkmoor was adopted late for military purposes, becoming an Observation, Aerial Reconnaissance and Photographic School, as well as an Aircraft Acceptance Park. Following the airfield's closure as a military establishment it was used for pleasure flights.

Tern Hill was requisitioned in 1916; a large flat area of over 300 acres on which contractors laid out two 1,000-yard grass landing strips, it became No. 4 Training Depot Station (TDS). By 1917, No. 34 and 43 Reserve Squadrons of the Royal Flying Corps arrived for training, using mainly the AVRO 504's and Sopwith Camels aircraft. Later the units were renumbered and Tern Hill became No. 13 TDS. Towards the end of the war, it became a bomber training station but with the Armistice this ceased to be developed and the base was closed in 1922.

Types of aeroplanes, from Great Britain, America, France, Italy and Germany, in use at the time of the First World War. (Author's collection)

Shawbury, probably one of the oldest military airfields in the north-west of England, saw its origins in 1915, when land west of Shawbury village was requisition, much to the annoyance of a

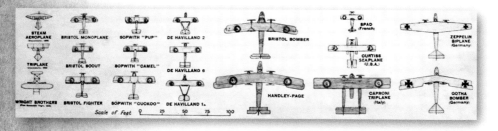

number of local farmers. The contractors, MacAlpines, levelled the ground, cleared away fences and filled in ditches, before laying out grass runways. A shortage of labour saw Irish navies brought in assisted by German prisoners of war.

By the summer of 1917, Shawbury was complete and became the headquarters of No. 29 Training Wing, a unit of the Australian Flying Corps (in the later renumbering Shawbury became No. 9 TDS). The wing was made up of five squadrons, three based at Shawbury and two at Tern Hill and the entire wing was commanded by Major A.W. Tedder, often known today as the 'Father of the Royal Air Force'. On 1 September 1917, an Aeroplane Repair Section was formed, although besides maintaining and repairing aircraft it also received and issued them to squadrons.

In November 1917 the first Americans arrived to join the British and Australian trainee pilots. Their attitude was easy going and discipline was not as strict; they had been known to take girlfriends for flights. When a Sopwith Camel crash-landed on the Newport Grammar School playing field it was said to be an American pilot on his way back from seeing his girlfriend! There were reports of aircraft flying under the bridges of Shrewsbury and James McCudden, one of a family of famous pilots, may possibly have been responsible.

In January 1918, Canadian, South African and New Zealand airmen began to arrive at Shawbury for training. What the villagers of Shawbury thought of these cosmopolitan arrivals into a community which up to 1915 had no electricity, no running water and no drains is not recorded, but they were all invited to the concerts and films that were put on in the canvas hangers. Portable generators had been brought in to supply electricity, although communications to the station were still primitive. There was no direct telegraph connection to Whitehall so important messages were sent to the village post office and a messenger would then take it by hand to the station.

Unfortunately accidents were common. The need for pilots meant that inexperienced instructors pushed pupils through very short flying courses as quickly as possible. Three Americans were killed in accidents at Shawbury and buried in St Mary's parish church in the village; Private L.G. Houseal, who died on 1 October 1918; Private O. Kious, 13 November 1918 and George Roper, 25 May 1918. The bodies of the two former men were later repatriated to the United States. George, a 2nd Lieutenant in the RAF, was one of a number of young Americans who had been serving with the Royal Flying Corps prior to the USA entering the conflict.

At the end of the war Shawbury was closed, the buildings demolished and the land returned to agricultural use. It was reinstated, along with Tern Hill, by the end of the 1930s and both are still in military hands today.

Concentration or Internment Camps

Almost as soon as war was declared the authorities issued instructions that any foreigners resident in Britain should be sent to internment camps. In Oakengates the local newspaper reported that 'great excitement was manifest' in the town as a number of Germans who were employed by the Lilleshall Company returned to Germany. The first prisoner-of-war camp to be opened in Shropshire was in the grounds of the dismantled Midland Wagon Works at Coleham in Shrewsbury; the premises were enclosed by strong barbed wire which was said to be electrically charged.

ENLISTMENT NUMBERS From the date of mobilisation to 31 December 1914, it was estimated that 4,628 men in Shropshire had joined the Reservists and Territorials and, during January 1915, there was an average of thirty-three men per day enlisting.

By September 1914, the camp was being prepared for the accommodation of both captured German prisoners of war and resident foreign nationals. The *Gloucester Journal* reported that, on 26 October 1914, 'enemy aliens' of military age from that county had been sent to Shrewsbury. Ernest Koanig, who escaped from Shrewsbury in November 1914, had been a resident in England for some time. He said he found the gates open and walked out because he wanted to see his wife and children who lived in Liverpool.

The International Red Cross, when it inspected the Shrewsbury camp, found the prisoners well fed and in good spirits. However, the camp commander Colonel Cholmondeley, in an open letter dated December 1914, stated that 'the soldiers [note not prisoners] were destitute having only their uniform to wear since August and no money to buy tobacco or food to supplement their daily ration'. The colonel gave them permission to hold a Christmas concert within the camp to raise funds; tickets would be sold at 3s, 2s or 6d corresponding to the seating. This, he said, would also benefit the men by occupying them in its preparation. The idea appears to have been accepted locally and was supported by the Mayor of Shrewsbury, however, the reaction in the national press was very different. It was 'nothing short of an insult' and the 'widespread feeling that the tendency to pamper them is deplorable in view of the needs of our men at the front' reported a number of national newspapers. The *Evening Standard* of 16 December 1914 thought that, in any event, the 'entertainment' provided by the Teuton prisoner (even though he should be a man of 'kultur') was 'hardly likely to be worth anything like the amount so coolly demanded'. The War Office eventually intervened and vetoed the concert.

Despite the banning of the concert, permission was given to a group of German ladies to provide a traditionally decorated Christmas tree for the camp. It was also reported that on the Wednesday before Christmas, a German lady and her chauffeur arrived with a car 'well-laden with gifts' for each of the prisoners.

Not all those living nearby resented the camp and its prisoners: a maid in a nearby house was arrested under the Defence of the Realm Act (DORA) for communicating with them – it was alleged that she ran a 'secret Post Office'. Police, having observed 'a good deal of signalling … between the females in the house and the German prisoners in the compound', then watched as a letter was picked up from under a brick just outside the wire of the camp. On investigation, further letters were discovered in the maid's room; both the maid and her employer stated there was no intention of helping the prisoners to escape, the letters were written as 'merely friendship'. Both ladies were fined.

Dame Agnes Hunt and the Baschurch Home Hospital

Florence House was originally opened as a convalescent home for disabled children by Agnes Hunt, with a committee of friends and family. Agnes established the principle of 'open-air' treatment, adopting the known benefits of fresh air and erecting wards within the grounds as open-sided sheds.

At the outbreak of war the hospital offered thirty-five beds for the use of wounded soldiers and, throughout August and September of 1914, new **Voluntary Aid Detachment** (VAD) nurses were taught the art of nursing. By that autumn, as no patients had been received, the War Office was contacted and on 27 November at 3.00 p.m., the hospital was informed that 'under no circumstances would the … beds [be required] … as they had sufficient'. At 5.00 p.m. that same day a telegram told the hospital to meet thirty wounded soldiers off the train and at about 10.00 p.m. the first wounded men arrived.

The hospital became an official auxiliary military establishment in August 1916 and, at a request for more beds, the War Office sent five large marquees which remained in place until June 1919. Throughout the war children were still being accepted at the hospital. Funded by Shropshire County Council, Agnes claimed them to be 'the first public body in the world' to accept the responsibility of the disabled child.

In 1919 the British Red Cross Society helped towards the funding of a new hospital; the old Park Hall Military Hospital near Oswestry was purchased and Shropshire Orthopaedic Hospital at Gobowen was born.

Agnes Hunt was awarded the Royal Red Cross in 1918 in recognition of her work during the First World War and, in 1926, she was created dame. Known as the pioneer of orthopaedic nursing, Dame Agnes Hunt died in 1948 at the age of 82.

A comic postcard of a military hospital ward. (Ironbridge Gorge Museum Trust)

Hospitals

At the time of the Great War there was no overall National Health Service in place, instead the welfare of the nation was still under the province of the Poor Law Amendment Act of 1834. In general the care of the sick and poor came under the parish, overshadowed by the Union Workhouses whose administration was in the hands of a Board of Guardians. Any medical care, from doctor, nurse or midwife, had to be paid for; those who were able had insurance cover and some industrial companies and trade unions organised 'Clubs' where the employees contributed a small amount each week in order to cover medical expenses.

In 1900 the Lilleshall Company of Priorslee had their own hospital paid for and operated by the company, having eight beds, a nursing sister and a female attendant with the local practioner Dr McCarthy as consultant. Other hospitals in the county were supported by wealthy patrons, such as the Lady Forester hospitals in Broseley and Much Wenlock, or by charitable funds. Admittance to these hospitals usually depended on referrals from local doctors; some workhouses also established infirmaries where the sick, unable to pay for medical care would get treatment provided by their parish.

A rare photograph of Betton Strange House during the First World War, with the ambulance and driver posed in front. (Kindly loaned by Brian Curran)

Betton Strange.

Within weeks of the outbreak of war, wounded soldiers started to arrive back in Britain, with many coming to Shropshire for their care and recuperation. The county had a large number of country houses and some of the owners generously made them available as nursing and convalescence homes. In 1915, the Dowager Countess of Dudley offered Hawkstone Park as a hospital for officers; having a large swimming bath, extensive grounds and tennis courts it was an 'ideal house for the purpose' and was 'much appreciated by its patients'.

By 1 January 1915, seven auxiliary hospitals were already opened and occupied: Cygnfeld, Baschurch, Attingham Park, Oakley Manor, Essex House in Church Stretton, Quarry Place and Shavington. Oakley Manor, near Newport, was converted into a hospital. It was able to accommodate forty-eight patients in seven wards, together with an outside ward for the 'benefits of open–air treatment'. The vinery had been converted to a dining room, with the coach houses transferred into workshops. The commandant was Miss C.E. Hughes and Mrs Scott Deakin was the quarter-master, secretary and treasurer. There were two qualified hospital nurses and about fifty VAD nurses, together with a couple of doctors.

The county's civilian hospitals also allocated beds for wounded soldiers: Royal Salop Infirmary; Eye, Ear & Throat, in Shrewsbury; the Lady Forester hospitals at Broseley and Much Wenlock; the Cottage Hospital, Oswestry; the Cottage Hospital, Whitchurch; the Cottage Hospital, Wellington and the Infirmary at Bridgnorth all opened their doors to those injured in the war. The Royal Salop Infirmary offered the use of its X-ray equipment, which at the time was the most up to date, free of charge to the auxiliary hospitals.

In May 1916 the War Office took over the buildings and hospital at Berrington (originally the site of the Shrewsbury and Atcham Workhouse) and from September of that year it was designated a military hospital. Berrington War Hospital, as it would become, accommodated around 400 patients and served as an administration centre for Shropshire and adjoining counties. There were also military hospitals at both the

Park Hall Camp, Oswestry and at Prees Heath, and by May 1918 there were said to be 1,336 beds for the wounded in Shropshire, excluding the Berrington War Hospital and the Wellington Infirmary. Wounded soldiers were dressed in blue 'uniforms' and Ethel Hudson remembers her dad being given special leave because she had to go into hospital to have her tonsils out; there were 'a lot of soldiers there convalescing wearing light blue suits, I was very spoilt by the soldiers who gave me sweets'.

On arrival in Britain, wounded servicemen were generally sent to a county-based hospital for assessment. However, in Shropshire, the ambulance trains arrived in Shrewsbury straight from Southampton or Dover. With no national or county ambulance service available to collect wounded men from these trains, the locality relied on volunteers to loan their private vehicles for this purpose. Mr and Mrs Logan of Overley helped obtain a Panhard Landaulette which was converted into a four-stretcher ambulance and a number of local tradesmen loaned their commercial vehicles. Gradually various organisations began to fund and donate ambulances, the people of Shrewsbury, for example, raised enough to purchase a vehicle and it was presented to the Volunteer Ambulance Corps.

A ward in a military hospital and, judging by the decorations, the picture was taken at Christmas time. Some of the men are still in bed but those that are up and dressed are in the blue 'uniform' of the wounded soldier. (Ironbridge Gorge Museum Trust)

Companies were also willing to help out and the officials and workmen from various departments of the Lilleshall Company and the Shropshire Miners' Federation each donated an ambulance to the Red Cross Society and St John's Ambulance Association. Each vehicle, reported the *Wellington Journal*, 'cost £600, is admirably equipped, commodious and comfortable, [and] constitute a handsome tribute to the generosity … of those who contributed to their purchase'. The ambulances were presented on New Year's Day 1916, following a parade through the streets of St Georges and led by the St Georges' Temperance Band. The opportunity was also taken to collect funds for the Red Cross Society, a 'duty undertaken by a contingent of young ladies, fascinatingly costumed and irresistibly endowed with graceful persuasiveness' who raised over £39.

When the wounded arrived at Shrewsbury station it was usually in the early hours of the morning and the men often had to wait to be sent on to other hospitals. During this time, a Mrs Davies and her assistants at the Railwaymen's Refreshment Room provided tea and sandwiches; whilst another group of ladies led by Mrs Urwick would be on hand to attend with blankets and pillows once the train arrived, all often having to wait for

Stretcher cases being loaded into an 'ambulance'. A far cry from the modern purpose-built ambulances of today, nonetheless these vehicles were vital for transporting wounded men from railway station to hospital and between hospitals. (Kindly loaned by Jim Cooper)

Ambulance donated by the Shropshire Miners' Federation to the combined British Red Cross and St John's Ambulance Association. This was presented on New Year's Day 1916 at St Georges following a parade through the streets. (Kindly loaned by Mr and Mrs J. Lowndes and Mr Jim Cooper)

hours through cold nights. This was occurring throughout the county, at other railway stations. On 27 July 1916, for instance, twenty-six wounded soldiers, including ten stretcher cases, arrived at Ironbridge to be taken to Broseley Forester Cottage Hospital by members of the Volunteer Transport Corps (VTC).

Refreshments were provided at the station by Mrs Randall, the postmistress, together with Mrs Howells, and as the newspaper noted, their thoughtfulness was appreciated by all the soldiers.

Nursing and Voluntary Aid Detachments

The hospitals established prior to the outbreak of war employed professionally trained nurses but the wartime auxiliary hospitals, in need of as many extra hands as possible, were generally worked by volunteer nurses overseen by trained professionals. During the early part

Captain McAlister rendered valuable service in the formation of the Shropshire VADs. He also worked strenuously to develop the Shropshire National Reserve, which consisted of ex-servicemen. In August 1914 it had a muster roll of 1,500 whose services were immediately available for duty. (Wellington Journal and Shrewsbury News, 4 May 1929)

of the war, Shropshire's Red Cross Society and St John's Ambulance Association amalgamated and, together with the VADs, provided the majority of the nursing staff in these auxiliary hospitals.

By 1914 the VADs movement in Shropshire was established and, by January 1915, there were twenty-four detachments (or groups) with a further six to come. There was also a reserve group, which was the administrative arm of the VADs and, besides the office paperwork, this reserve also dealt with the local volunteers. The exact number of nurses working in

ROMANCE BLOSSOMS
Miss Eleanor Jacson, a skilled nursing sister at the Oakley Manor VAD hospital, offered her services as soon as the war broke out. Whilst caring for Sergeant Archibald Cree, who had received serious injuries whilst fighting in Flanders, a 'warm attachment had manifest itself'. The couple married in July 1915.

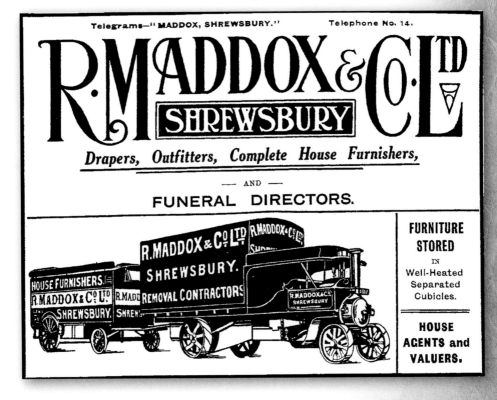

An advert from 1917 for R. Maddox & Co. Ltd, a department store in Shrewsbury who, along with the similar store Della Porter's, supported the war. They sold necessities for the VAD nurses, such as aprons, stocked bandages and often had fund-raising days when a percentage of the profits were given to the war effort. (Kelly Trade Directory, 1917)

CHURCH STRETTON WAR HOSPITAL SUPPLY DEPOT
Throughout the war this depot had supplied many items, amongst which were: bandages, swabs of all kinds, eye pads, pneumonia jackets, sphagnum moss, dressings, splints, pressure pads and papier mâché slings.

Shropshire hospitals remains difficult to assess as numbers fluctuated and those nurses sent direct from Devonshire House, the headquarters of the VADs, were not included in local figures.

Some ladies started out as volunteers but went on to serve in the military hospitals where they had accommodation, a grant for a uniform and a small salary, although during the war a small allowance towards lodging, laundry and uniform could be granted. A large number of the ladies who volunteered were not members of any of the nursing organisations but helped where they could; some who were employed in shops gave an hour before work, whilst others would devote their Sundays to assisting in the hospitals despite working during the week.

There were five Men's Detachments at the beginning of the war, though their numbers generally dwindled as members enlisted or were called up and no new detachments were formed. The Shrewsbury Detachment managed to avoid this trend and actually increased its numbers, due, in the main, to the 'untiring energy' of ambulance officer Percy Allen.

Financing and servicing both the hospitals and the nursing staff was a constant problem for the administration staff, especially as the cost of supplies and the number of hospitals increased. By 1917 negotiations with the War Office resulted in a rise in the amount of grant received by the hospitals of up to 3s 3d per day for every patient, plus another 6d a day for every bed that was unoccupied. This extra money allowed the county committee to form a Reserve Fund to cover repairs should damage occur to houses rented during the war period. Accommodation, especially in Shrewsbury, for the volunteer nurses who came from outside the county was becoming more difficult and it was decided in 1916 that a hostel was the best solution. Eventually the money was raised and a hostel was established in Shrewsbury Quarry.

In 1915 Mr Novis, as Honorary Secretary to the Shropshire Voluntary Aid Detachment Committee, developed a card-index system in order to keep track of all the men admitted to the hospitals. The County Director, Mr Swire, explained the system in his report and described how, when an ambulance train arrived, a list of the patients was sent to the Berrington War Hospital with a copy forwarded to the committee. The name and regimental number of each man, together with the date and name of the hospital to which he was sent, was then entered on a card. When the man was moved or discharged, the details would be added to the card, thus enabling the man to be traced when relatives asked for information. Mrs Rowan-Robinson, together with a number of ladies, helped in the administration of this system and by the end of 1917 over 12,600 cards were kept.

AMBULANCE TRAINS
The number of ambulance trains and the number of wounded men arriving at Shropshire stations were reported as follows: 'In 1915 there were 12 trains with 1666 men; in 1916, 18 trains with 2,838 men and in 1917, 46 trains with 6,459 men.'

3

WORK OF WAR

During the miners' strikes and industrial unrest of 1912 and 1913, men (and often their families too) could be seen digging for coal on old spoil heaps. In this photograph at Benthall Woods, near Broseley the men seem to be more organised, how many would soon be going to war? (Ironbridge Gorge Museum Trust)

Prior to the outbreak of the war there had been a number of years of industrial unrest and, from 1910, a series of strikes were organised; the miners' strike of 1912 caused particular hardship amongst those living on the east Shropshire coalfield. The declaration of war brought a general cessation of industrial troubles as both employers and employees joined together in the war effort.

Initially agriculture, industry and commercial enterprises supported and encouraged their employees to enlist, believing in the contemporary propaganda that 'it would all be over by Christmas'. On 25 September 1914, the Duke of Sutherland, in an address to his Lilleshall estate workers, urged them to join up and promised to keep their places open. He went on to say that he would care for the wives and dependents of those who

enlisted and would not ask for any payment of rent. The duke also stated that he undertook 'that any man who loses either his life or limb he will make himself responsible for the payment of an allowance to the man himself or his dependents'. Messrs Maw & Co., tile manufacturers of Jackfield, offered all their employees who enlisted a month's wages and a promise that their jobs would remain open on their return, whilst R. Maddox, a large department store in Shrewsbury, gave each of their eight employees who were in the reserves two blankets, two shirts, and two pairs of socks.

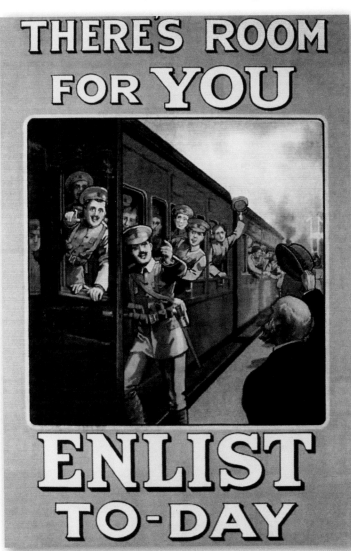

An enlistment poster. (Author's collection)

A selection of enlistment posters. The need for more men became increasingly acute and Lord Kitchener organised a colourful poster campaign to encourage volunteers. (Kindly loaned by Mr R.B. Simpson)

However, as the war progressed into a second year, it became clear that supplying men for the conflict and continuing to produce both armaments and food would not be achievable.

Agriculture

Britain had grown to depend on the importation of foodstuffs, especially corn, so when the increasingly successful German U-boat campaigns in the Atlantic began to restrict these food imports an increase in home production was vital. Counties organised War Agricultural Committees in order to administer the supply of labour, examine food supplies and report on shortages as they occurred. A number of smallholders had formed a co-operative in order to bulk buy seeds, fertiliser, etc. and the committee advised them that loans were available on application to the Agricultural Organisation Society in London.

During harvest time the shortage of labour was particularly acute; in certain circumstances the military authorities granted extended leave to soldiers for agricultural duties and even temporarily released soldiers from the military. Farmers were advised to apply to the local Agricultural Distribution Centre in Shrewsbury if they wanted to retain the services of any military men. In 1917 some thirty-seven applications had been received by farmers to keep their soldier labourers, especially as some were already experienced farmhands and others were undergoing training. Schoolchildren from this period later recalled how, during the summer and autumn, groups of soldiers would help farmers with the harvest and potato

VOLUNTEERS FOR HAY-MAKING. — Owing to the shortage of labour in the fields due to the Army's requisitions, some 30 of the Wellington High School boys have volunteered to assist in the hay-making in their own district. Their offer is, in all cases, made with their parents' consent, and has been welcomed in many quarters. Food for the day is the only return the boys ask. They will be sent in small parties where their help is asked for.

The local newspaper called for volunteers for haymaking. (Wellington Journal and Shrewsbury News, *1917*)

picking whilst being billeted in homes in their villages. Help was called upon from all quarters and members of the local community chipped in as well as they could. In August 1914, the Revd C.A. Almington (headmaster of Shrewsbury School) announced that, owing to the shortage of labour, he intended to undertake work in the harvest field.

By 1917 the labour shortage in agriculture was such that the Newport War Agriculture Committee was asked to consider bringing in German prisoners of war to help on the farms. A village schoolboy recalled that, in 1918, six German prisoners were brought in to help with the harvest in his village: 'All the women and children turned out to see them, the women had mops and brooms and shouted at them and the guards escorting the prisoners told the women to calm down.' He was asked to lead the horses for them and remembers being terrified. Then Mr Williams (the supervisor) put the prisoners to work, two on the waggon and four to pitch the sheaves up on the back: 'They introduced themselves to me I did not think they could speak English so I was surprised. On the second day they gave me 3*d* to get some beer from the pub. They showed us photos of their families and before long the same women who had shouted at them were giving them jugs of tea and cake.'

The government, under the auspices of the Shropshire War Agricultural Committee, made equipment, horses and labour available for farmers to hire, including six Howard Champion ploughs and six Brown and Sons ploughs. At a 1917 meeting it was reported that ploughs were charged at 1*s* 6*d* per day, horses at 5*s* 6*d* per day per horse and men at 5*s* per day per man; they had thirty-five horses out with farmers and about ten men available for work and there were twenty-two tractors working in the county.

In rural areas the wives and families of agricultural labourers had always worked on the land, particularly on the dairy and poultry side but also assisting at haymaking and harvest times. As both labour and food shortages increased many middle-class women felt the need to 'do their bit' and in 1917 the Board of

Agricultural set up the Women's Land Army (WLA) in order to 'increase the supply of women workers on the land'. The WLA was divided into three sections: Agriculture, Forage (animal feed) and Timber Cutting and each county had a Women's War Agricultural Committee who, besides keeping a register of the available women workers, encouraged farmers to employ these women.

Between March 1917 and May 1919, 23,000 women had passed through the WLA training centres and became full-time land girls. They worked in a variety of occupations and although the majority were employed in milking or as field workers, a few specialised in horse ploughing or tractor driving.

Harper Adams Agricultural College

'Making Girl Farmers'
Harper Adams Agricultural College was established in 1901 on an estate near Newport 'for the purpose of teaching practical and theoretical agriculture'. It initially opened with six students and offered certificated practical courses and a longer college diploma course. The significant feature of the college was its own 178-acre farm, to which a specialist poultry unit was added in 1909.

A photograph showing various farm transport machinery, tractors, steam engines, caterpillar-tracked vehicles and their drivers at Harper Adams Agricultural College, 1918. There are a number of girls included which suggests this was a course in the maintenance and driving of these vehicles. (Ironbridge Gorge Museum Trust)

NO HEALTH AND SAFETY
One woman remembered her aunt who had worked at a munitions factory which made poisonous gas: 'She was taken ill ... and put on a train back to Wem alone, when she arrive at home she lived just 2 weeks, she was only 20.'

An article in Ladies Pictorial, *5 June 1915, showed the girls in the poultry department digging and hoeing, bringing in the sheep and lambs and feeding the pigs.* (Ladies Pictorial, *June 1915)*

Student numbers were to gradually increase, reaching an all-time high in the 1910–11 session, but unsurprisingly there was a fall in both staff and student numbers after 1914. This reduced income produced a financial burden which had forced a number of similar institutions to close during the war, but Harper Adams Agricultural College managed to remain open throughout. The staff continued to work, giving some 751 lectures and demonstrations at day and evening centres to a total audience of well over 16,000.

In the spring of 1915, the college arranged two short courses in 'the lighter branches of agriculture' to train sixty women, becoming the first institution to run such courses. At the end of the courses most of the students were able to find employment earning between 10s and 16s a week. In the 1916–17 session, 131 students enrolled on short courses and of these students 128 were women. The following session, running 1917–18, also saw high numbers of female applicants with ninety-two members of the Women's Land Army being trained at the college. As war reduced the number of horses

available for agricultural work it spurred on the introduction of tractors and machinery; around fifty-five women trained as tractor drivers and some of the first of these to qualify were sent to plough up the Old Trafford Racecourse in Manchester. The college secretary remarked, 'I think we can safely say these girls mean business.'

As well as an educational establishment, the college was also involved in a number of experiments and trials in agricultural developments. One of the most successful was the poultry egg-laying trials: established in 1912 they led to the availability of day-old chicks for sale. This was initiated by the Board of Agriculture and ensured that both smallholders and householders could purchase good quality poultry at a relatively low price.

Under the administration of the principle, the college Hedworth Foulkes became involved in the organisation of preserving fruit. In 1916 there had been a large local damson harvest so around 120 women were organised and, using the facilities of the Springfield Brewery in Newport, produced about 18 tons of pulped fruit a day to be used in making jam for the army.

Industry

The local iron and steel manufacturers were, of course, vital to the war effort and a number of the heavy engineering businesses were eventually taken into government control. The Coalbrookdale Company announced that the works were under government control on 8 November 1914 and Charles Peskin noted that the Union Jack was hoisted on that day. Normal work was diverted to the manufacture of aerial bombs, hand grenades, gun carriage brake blocks and various types of light engineering castings. By 1915 the production of gates and railings ceased and the Severn Foundry, built in 1901 to meet new demands, was closed in 1917 due to the shortage of manpower lost to war services; the engineering department was then leased to the Liverpool Refrigeration Company which retained it until 1929.

Women and girls working on the munitions at the Coalbrookdale Works with their (male) supervisor: the girls have chalked messages on the bombs, 'A Present for the Kaiser', 'To Berlin' and 'A Pill for Fritz'. This was not at all unusual; the workers at munition works all over Britain were sending similar messages. (Ironbridge Gorge Museum Trust)

Winifred Egan remembered that after 'all the boys had gone' girls began to be employed in a number of jobs, working on average from 7.30 a.m. to 5.00 p.m. She added that 'Some of the girls riveted, some cleaned the bombs and some painted them', the bombs were then assembled ready to be shipped out. Betty Duddell recalled that her mother worked as a crane driver in the engineering shop and as she had to climb ladders to get into the crane she wore trousers. 'I was so disgusted to see a photograph with my mother wearing trousers when I was a child. I tore it out of a photograph album!'

A committee was established to advise on the supply of explosives and Lord John Fletcher Moulton (1844–1921), of Madeley, Shropshire was appointed as chairman. Although 70 years of age, Lord Moulton used his expertise to help guide the Explosive Supply Department (ESD) to become a useful branch of the War Office, responsible for the manufacture of high explosives and propellants. By the end of the war ESD was turning out 1,000 tons of high explosives a day. It was said that Lord Moulton worked a ten-hour day and took less than ten days' holiday during the entire four years of the war. He also personally visited every munitions factory. In recognition of his services he was created KCB (Knight Commander of the Bath) in 1915; GCB (Grand Commander of the Bath) in 1917 and received the Etoile Noir of France, the Order of Leopold (Belgium) and was the final receiver of the Order of the White Eagle before the Russian Monarchy collapsed.

In 1910 Joseph Sankey & Sons had taken over the Hadley Castle Works and had been manufacturing motor parts but as a government-controlled establishment they had to diversify into war production. They manufactured field kitchens, mine hemispheres, wagons, paravanes (a device to cut the moorings of submerged mines) and smoke-making apparatus. In 1917 the *Journal* reported that the company allowed its 'munition girl workers … in their khaki overalls' to take part in the Hadley Carnival procession.

Lord Moulton (1844–1921). (LC-DIG-ggbain-13509)

Small industrial concerns that did not come under government control also diversified into war work. Audley Engineering, a small engineering works located in Newport, evolved from specialising in the manufacture of a variety of valves and valve equipment to making anchor plummets for mine sinkers with over eighty employees, including girls, working in their machine shop during the war.

Messrs Thomas & Sons of Oswestry had obtained important government contracts to supply horseshoe boxes, but the demand and shortages of 'boy labour' was proving a problem. However, help was at hand as the local newspaper reported:

> … the ladies … were chiefly old public school with time on their hands every day. Here where all were unaccustomed to manual labour, but the spur of patriotism was sufficient to induce them to turn out at 6.00 a.m. on Monday morning and take their places at the mill … They work 2 shifts are paid for their services and [they are] proving very capable workers.

Messrs Corbett's of both Wellington and Shrewsbury had made agricultural machinery and implements, with Wellington specialising in the production of small corn-grinding mills. This work continued throughout the war as the shortage of labour created a demand for all 'labour-saving' machinery.

The collieries throughout Shropshire remained open and, as coal was a vital fuel, miners were exempt from military service although large numbers did volunteer. In the later years of the war the lack of labour in the pits caused coal shortages and the War Office agreed to release ex-miners serving in the military. It was reported that some were reluctant, for fear they would be seen as 'shirkers', but the newspaper reassured them it was 'their patriotic duty' as the 'country was threatened with a very serious shortage of fuel'. The coal shortage also gave the opportunity for small coal pits to be opened; two new coal pits opened in the Horsehay area appeared to be flourishing and in the Lawley district it was said that a man had commenced to sink a coal pit in his garden.

Both Randlay and Hadley Brickworks announced that they required women and girls to do the light clay work. The *Dawley News* stated that it attracted a great crowd of local applicants but posed the question 'Will the older men strike?' inferring perhaps that not all welcomed the prospect of female fellow workers.

> When Jack left school his first job was filling bags of coal for the Wellington Coal Company, but this did not go down too well. His dad advised him to join the Great Western Railway then 'he would still have a job when the war finished'. Mr Hogg, who offered Jack a job, reputedly told him: 'Don't be like these other fools and join up, I can find you a job.'
>
> *Jack Edwards, born 1901*

Not all soldiers worked on the land; about fifty soldiers from the Durham Regiment were employed at the Hollinswood crusher helping to turn out ballast. They were billeted in Oakengates and St Georges and could be seen in their khaki overalls parading at the beginning of each day under the direction of Lieutenant C.J. Ruffle. Similarly, it was not just ex-miners who were recalled from the front. A few soldiers returned home for the purpose of working on munitions and the *Dawley News* gives an example in 1916 of an 'iron-turner' put through a test at his base and drafted home to serve in a workshop.

New concerns also moved into the area, Messrs Johnson Brothers of Harborne, Birmingham purchased the Wesleyan School Hall in Wellington for the purpose of a toy factory. They were to produce teddy bears and other soft goods that had previously been imported from Germany, and were able to offer employment to around sixty girls.

The decorative ceramics concerns in the Ironbridge Gorge area suffered an almost immediate loss of trade from the United States and from a number of their German clients. The following letter, received by the Coalport China Works from one of their German contacts, speaks for itself:

> I regret to have to inform you that owing to the perfidious way of acting of the English government towards the German people all business connextions [*sic*] with England must be discontinued and I herewith wish to inform you that I cancel all commands not yet executed and shall in facture not pass you any further orders. All patriotic Germans will do likewise and England will have to return thanks for this commercial defeat to its excellent minister Mr Grey, whose speeches, [are] crammed full of lies and much acclaimed by loud cheers in Parliament. If the English public would have known positive facts and the truth, I am sure that all patriotic Englishmen would have acted quite otherwise. I shall take the liberty to send you from time to time true news, officially confirmed about the war and the German successes up to now, asking to spread same as much as possible so all English get aware how they have been betrayed by their Government. Yours faithfully Diedr. Lindemann.

Wellington Journal and Shrewsbury News, 14 November 1914

Maws, Craven Dunnill and the Coalport China Works all seem to have begun to produce souvenir type articles, decorated with patriotic symbols, along with a plainer type of utility wares.

In smaller concerns everyone in the community seemed to offer help. One instance saw the Revd Banbridge, Vicar of Atcham and a skilled motor mechanic, taking control of a large motor garage at Shrewsbury to fill the place of one of its proprietors, Mr Legge, the son of the late Bishop of Lichfield, who was serving in the army as a private. Mr Banbridge, the *Tamworth Herald* reported, 'is in daily attendance at the garage and has just organised a motor parcels express delivery, he also continued to take his usual Sunday services'.

An example of the many patriotic items produced during the war. This ceramic tile by Craven Dunnill is in full colour; at its centre are the flags of the Allies, Great Britain, Belgium, Russia and France, with figures of soldiers and sailors at opposite corners. (Ironbridge Gorge Museum Trust)

In the larger towns and cities there was an opportunity for women to become involved in a variety of occupations not previously available to them. Such opportunities were perhaps not quite so readily available in Shropshire, yet instances did occur and when, for example, Mr S. Phillips (the local Dawley postman) was called up, his work was 'done by a young lady'.

It was not just in paid employment that new opportunities arose: when Mr Connop, Master of the United Pack, was called up on active service, Miss Whitaker of Totterton Hall, Bishops Castle was appointed the Lady Master.

Tribunals

Despite the introduction of a number of voluntary enlistment schemes, Parliament judged that almost 500,000 single men who were fit for service had not yet volunteered. Consequently, 6 January 1916 saw the House of Commons come to the end of a lengthy debate and vote overwhelmingly for military conscription. Following this decision a system of tribunals was instigated along similar lines to a civil court, which meant that men who felt they were entitled to exemption from military service could put forward a case.

The tribunals were held before a committee of about twelve people, generally made up of local magistrates or alderman and usually with a military representative present. On hearing a case, and after due consideration, the committee then had the authority to issue appropriate exemption certificates. There were three types of certificate: absolute, conditional or temporary. Absolute exemption was rarely given at a tribunal, conditional exemption was given provided the appellant continued in his war work and a temporary certificate, which was the most common type issued, allowed the person to arrange his affairs before being drafted.

The usual requests for exemptions were for personal reasons, since conscription could arguably result in family hardship (especially if other members of the family had already joined up). This meant that a farmer, for example, received exemption for his fourth son if his other three sons were already in France. A smallholder is recorded to have requested a few extra weeks for his man until the hay was in; when asked by the chairman how long he required, the smallholder replied, 'Heaven knows – when it stops raining!'

In another case two brothers (both unmarried, aged 25 and 28), who were employed as shoeing smiths, claimed exemption on the grounds that they were engaged in shoeing horses for the colliery company and also making miners tools, as well as doing a great deal of work for local farmers. After due consideration the tribunal ordered the younger brother to join the army and granted a conditional exemption to the elder one.

At Dawley an interesting case came before the tribunal of two brothers employed in making footballs. The brothers produced documents which showed that the footballs were for a Paris firm that supplied them to the British and French troops; thereby showing that their occupation was serving a purpose in the war effort. Nevertheless, the committee felt that one of them ought to join up and it allowed them three months to decide who!

Sometimes an employer asked on behalf of an employee. A motor garage proprietor in Ironbridge, for instance, appealed on behalf of the only motorcar driver in his employment on the

NATIONAL AGRICULTURAL LABOURERS AND RURAL WORKERS UNION
A meeting of the Staffordshire and Shropshire branches protested at the increased employment of schoolchildren and women and urged the government to take control of the food supply.

Wellington Journal and Shrewsbury News, 27 March 1915

A photograph of the Horsehay Works about the time of the war. The Wrekin is visible in the background. (Ironbridge Gorge Museum Trust)

grounds that his services were indispensable. The proprietor added that he, himself, suffered from ill health and if this man left he would have to close his business. The clerk's reply was that the applicant would have to satisfy the tribunal that it was in the national interest for his business to continue. Although the applicant argued that his man was in the habit of assisting to convey wounded soldiers to local hospitals the application was refused.

On the whole, most men involved in the supply and provision of food – butchers, bakers and grocers – were granted conditional certificates, even a publican was allowed one as long as he signed on with the Ministry of Munitions. Regarding the men employed in government-controlled industrial premises, the situation regarding exemptions seems to have been far more complicated. In autumn 1916, thirteen men at the Horsehay Works had been 'de-badged' by the Ministry of Munitions, which meant they had to go into military service despite the support of the local tribunal for them to

remain in work. The company was forced to take their case to the Central Appeal Tribunal.

The tribunals were open to the public and a local newspaper editorial stated that most judgments seemed to be fair as the members of the tribunal have a thankless job and 'there is not a man on the tribunal therefore but would gladly give up this job to someone else'. Some members of the public did think that the big companies were treated too leniently and were 'able to secure exemption for all and sundry of their employees'. Even the *Daily Mail* suggested that the Dawley Tribunal was 'under the thumb of the farmer', but, as the *Dawley News* pointed out, there were no farmers on it!

Munitions Tribunals

Munitions Tribunals were more formal but less common; these heard appeals concerning Government Controlled Establishments and in 1917 the first one in the district was held at Wellington Police Court. The case concerned certificates of discharge, which were issued by a firm to any employee wishing to leave in order to work elsewhere. They were heard before a committee of assessors that included representatives of both the employer and the employee.

William Morgan and James Dunning, both from Dawley, were working as labourers for the Lilleshall Company. William stated his complaint that a 'certificate of discharge had been unreasonably withheld' by the company, a charge denied by Mr John Phillips, chief clerk of the Lilleshall Company's Engineering Department.

William was married with one child and had been employed at the New Yard for eight weeks on a wage of £1 1s 6d per week, which he found 'very hard to live upon'. He also had to walk 3.5 miles and so he looked for employment closer to home and was offered a place at the Horsehay Works at 23s per week, on production of a discharge certificate. William gave the required seven-day notice and applied for a certificate of discharge which was then refused.

LILLESHALL COMPANY

The Lilleshall Company was actively involved in a variety of trading activities: mining coal, ironstone, limestone and clay; making bricks and associated products; making and finishing iron and steel; and trading in light and heavy engineering. The company was also a major landowner, providing around 1,000 houses and cottages for its employees and caring for their welfare and education as well as providing its own public house, The Bird in Hand.

By the beginning of the twentieth century, the company was a prosperous concern in an international market and was involved with several German companies. This was the case at the New Yard, which became a specialist engineering works producing large gas engines under license from a Nuremberg company.

In 1914 most of the company's products were of value to the war effort and the German business involvement was immediately taken under government control, although it remained under Lilleshall Company management. The New Yard site, with its production facilities and engineering expertise, became a government-controlled establishment manufacturing thousands of shells.

In sites under government control the work force was, to some extent, protected from the call-up, however, other departments suffered from labour shortage. After management recommendations the Board implemented night-shift working and increased their employment of women.

With the economic slump that followed the end of the war, the Lilleshall Company were forced to make changes. Their mining department was especially hard hit and a number of collieries were closed, while both the steel and iron works had to reduce their hours. The brickworks and associated products did better, especially the production of the 'Belfast' sink for the locally built authority housing estates.

A department of the Lilleshall Company at Snedshill. The building is now demolished and the site is currently home to the stores Wickes and Aldi. (Ironbridge Gorge Museum Trust)

The employees of a department of the Lilleshall Company pose for a photograph, taken around 1913. (Ironbridge Gorge Museum Trust)

The Lilleshall Company's New Yard Engineering Department situated in Gower Street, St Georges. (Ironbridge Gorge Museum Trust)

The chairman of the tribunal then asked William why he had taken the work at Lilleshall, to which he replied that he had worked in Shrewsbury (where he probably had lodgings), and wanted to come home. Mr Phillips was then questioned by the chairman over the apparent difference in labourers' wages between Lilleshall and Horsehay. William, said Mr Phillips, received the district rate of pay, however, Horsehay was in a different district and the wages did not always agree.

After consultation with the other assessors, Mr Simmons concluded that Mr Morgan was entitled to a certificate of discharge as, 'labourers living in the vicinity [of the Lilleshall works] are better off than those living at a distance … the applicant is labouring under a hardship'.

The case of James Dunning reached the same conclusions and a certificate of discharge was granted.

The Police Force

On the outbreak of war, policemen throughout the country were amongst the first to enlist as many were ex-servicemen. At the time, Shropshire County had two distinct police forces: the Shropshire Constabulary and the Shrewsbury Borough Forces.

Police constables Weston and Kirk, both from Oswestry, were amongst the first to rejoin their regiments: the Royal Marine Artillery and the Oxford and Bucks Light Infantry respectively. The *Journal* reported that these 'young police officers with tact and courtesy had won the confidence of the public in the district and their comrades, an hour before their departure presented each with pipes, a cigarette case and a tobacco box'.

As the number of men in the police force decreased, special constables were brought in to assist and, at the same time, the concept of having women as police officers was gradually accepted throughout the country. In Shropshire the Shrewsbury Borough refused to even consider the employment of women, seeing them as unnecessary and impractical. The Shropshire Constabulary, however, took a very different view. On 11 March 1918, Sergeant Miss Emily Stephings and Constable Miss Isabella Napier Hardy commenced duty and were stationed at Whitchurch where their daily patrol duty consisted of two shifts of four hours each. The Whitchurch area was selected for this trial because of the close vicinity of the Prees Heath Military Camp, where women and girls frequented.

4

NEWS FROM THE FRONT LINE

Information regarding events and individual serving personnel during the conflict was, of course, subject to censorship. Letters sent by soldiers and the reports of war correspondents both received the 'blue pencil' treatment – blue pencils were used by the War Office to obliterate the words and phrases judged to give away too much detail. However, there were no such reporting restrictions in neutral countries, such as Spain, so news could often filter through to the British public.

Shropshire victim of the RMS Lusitania. (Shrewsbury Chronicle)

The war was brought closer to British shores when the RMS *Lusitania*, a British ocean liner, was torpedoed in a German U-boat attack on 7 May 1915, causing the death of over 1,100 passengers and crew. The liner had sailed from New York for Liverpool on 1 May 1915 and was packed with passengers: one of these was Mrs Bertha Prescott. Bertha had been born at Coreley, Shropshire and shortly after her marriage to George Prescott on 30 December 1912, the family had emigrated to Canada; she was returning to England to see her husband who had been invalided home from France.

The reality of war came directly into British homes as soldiers returned on leave, but most continued to believe that the

A small pocket-sized copy of St Luke's Gospel that was given to enlisted men. This was the personal copy belonging to Guardsman Ted Hough which he carried with him throughout his time in France. (Author's collection)

conflict was just. Bert Oakes wrote that 'greater things have to be done out here & God willing, the time will soon arrive when we shall all be "marching home again" to meet those left, & loved behind'. A religious upbringing was still strong in many families and most soldiers probably carried a bible or prayer book with them in the field.

Men from Shropshire

At the outbreak of war there were only two regular battalions of the King's Shropshire Light Infantry (KSLI). This rapidly expanded during the first month of the war to ten battalions, eight of which saw action.

There were also two volunteer mounted regiments, the Shropshire Yeomanry and the Royal Shropshire Horse Artillery. The Shropshire Yeomanry became an infantry regiment after 1917 and served in Egypt, Palestine and finally France. The Royal Shropshire Horse Artillery served throughout the war as Royal Field Artillery units.

Not all service personnel served in the mud of the trenches, Private W.E. Powell served with the Shropshire Yeomanry in Egypt. Writing to the *Dawley News* in 1916, he described the heat as 118 degrees in the shade and said that 'you would not know us in our khaki drill and dark glasses'. Like many young soldiers, it was Private Powell's first time out of Britain and the culture of the foreign lands was 'very interesting … they dress just as they did in Bible times … just like the pictures'. The country boy also observed that 'They have their yoke of oxen and plough and thresh corn just in the same way as we read in the Bible'.

The Plagues of Egypt keep the Shropshire Yeomanry in Constant Activity.

"The Flies and Mosquitoes are an awful pest."

Cartoon submitted to the Dawley News *by Private W.E. Powell serving in Egypt with the Shropshire Yeomanry. (*Dawley News, *June 1916. Kindly loaned by Mr Toby Neale)*

A Summary and Fatality From Those Battalions Who Saw Action

The 1st Battalion, prior to the outbreak of the war, had been based in Tipperary; they arrived in France in September 1914 with twenty-seven officers and 969 other ranks. The battalion fought in the First Battle of Ypres and played a leading part at Hooge in 1915. In April 1916 it was back at Ypres, where the battalion took part in some severe fighting and, on 24 April, their commanding officer, Lieutenant Colonel Luard DSO (Distinguished Service Order) was killed in action. Under Lieutenant Colonel Murray, 1st KSLI saw action at the Somme, at Arras and Cambrai. By early 1918, it was at the forefront against the German Spring Offensive and, within two days at Lagnicourt, was left with just over seventy men. The battalion reformed under Lieutenant Colonel Meynell and they were once again back at the front, taking part in the severe fighting on the Hindenburg Line. They stayed in France until the Armistice when they became part of the Rhineland occupation force, eventually returning to England in April 1919.

1st Battalion KSLI Private 12449 Francis J. Bowers was killed on 24 September 1918 during the Battle of the Hindenburg Line. He is buried in the Chapelle British Cemetery.

The 2nd Battalion had been stationed in India at the outbreak of the war but they returned to England and after training crossed to France. By April 1915, under Lieutenant Colonel Bridgford, they were fighting in the Second Battle of Ypres and, in October, were ordered to Macedonia, arriving in Salonika in December 1915. The battalion spent nearly three years fighting on the Struma Front, where Lieutenant G.K. Lloyd, a valuable officer, died of appendicitis on 21 February 1916. During the course of the war in France twelve officers and around 287 other ranks were killed in action or died as a result of wounds, disease or injuries, whilst during the time spent in Macedonia sixty-seven men were lost. The battalion finally arrived back in Shrewsbury on 2 July 1919.

2nd Battalion KSLI Private 16796 Samuel Harris from Madeley died in hospital on 20 December 1916. Probably a victim of malaria, he is buried in the Salonika (Lemet Road) Military Cemetery, Greece.

Immediately prior to the outbreak of the war, the 4th Battalion (Territorial Army) was at an annual training camp at Glan Rheidol, near Aberystwyth; by 4 August 1914 they had left Shrewsbury in two special trains for Barry Docks near Cardiff. In December 1914, the battalion arrived in India and then travelled on to the Far East, returning to Plymouth on 27 July 1917 via South Africa and Sierra Leone. Two days later, without being granted the expected leave, they were disembarking at Le Havre. The battalion was awarded the Croix de Guerre avec Palme for its gallantry in the successful attack at Bligny Hill on 6 June 1918, and finally arrived home in Southampton on 18 May 1919.

YOUNG VOLUNTEERS

The young volunteers knew nothing of the horrors to come: 'I often remember before we went to the Battle of Passendale we had a bit of a service and the Colonel talked to us and he cried, he knowed what we was going in for – it was hell!'

Len Edwards,
Private in the KSLI

The eight casualties of the Far East all died of disease, whilst in France eleven officers were killed and seventy-seven wounded; of the other ranks, 353 were killed, died of wounds, disease or accident and 1,260 were wounded. In addition to this about seventy were taken prisoner, of whom three died whilst in captivity.

3rd Battalion KSLI Private 200437 Samuel Rigby was one of eight soliders who succumbed to disease. He died of fever on 14 July 1917 and is buried in the Freetown (King Tom) Cemetery, Sierra Leone.

The 5th Battalion was raised on 6 August 1914 under Lieutenant Colonel H.M. Smith and was the first of the KSLI battalions to be formed during the war. After training in Aldershot, the battalion landed in France in May 1915 and served entirely on the Western Front. Heavily engaged throughout the war, especially in 1916 at Delville Wood and Flers-Courcelette, the 5th Battalion served until February 1918 when it was suddenly disbanded and its personnel distributed amongst other KSLI battalions.

5th Battalion KSLI Lance Corporal 17534 Frederick Austin of Madeley was killed in action on 24 August 1916 at Delville Wood. He is remembered on the Thiepval Memorial.

The 6th Battalion left the depot in Shrewsbury for Blackdown, Dorset on 10 September 1914. Led by Lieutenant Colonel S.G. Moor, they were posted to France in July 1915 and served on the Western Front. Towards the end of 1917 the battalion saw action near Cambrai and, during the German Spring Offensive of 1918, it was involved in severe fighting at St Quentin. Following the end of the war they returned to Shrewsbury and disbanded in 1919.

This battalion became known as a 'Pals Regiment' as its companies consisted of friends, colleagues or workmates who were encouraged to serve together. 'C' Company, for example, was made up almost entirely of Shrewsbury friends. The practice was soon abandoned, however, particularly after the Somme when many companies were decimated. The community of Accrington in Lancashire, which had its own 'Accrington Pals', lost 584 of the 720 men who enlisted with their local regiment in this way.

WANTED.
EXPERT TELEGRAPHISTS OR SIGNALLERS.
with First-class Certificate for Service, with
THE SIGNAL TROOP OF THE WELSH BORDER MOUNTED BRIGADE.
WILL ONLY BE ACCEPTED IF WILLING TO UNDERTAKE FOREIGN SERVICE.
Apply,
O.C., SIGNAL TROOP, W.B.M.B.,
ECCLESTON CAMP, CHESTER.

An advert to encourage recruits with specialist training, but only if they are willing to serve overseas. The fighting battalions required more fighting men as the casualty numbers continued to mount. (Wellington Journal and Shrewsbury News)

6th Battalion KSLI Lance Corporal Albert Davies of Ketley Bank died as a prisoner of war at Kassel on 8 August 1918 and is buried in the Niederzwehren Cemetery, Hessen, Germany.

The 7th Battalion, formed in Shrewsbury in September 1914 under Lieutenant Colonel J.H. Barber, arrived in France in September 1915; it was at Ypres during the winter of 1915–16 and saw action at the Somme in July 1916. They were at Arras in the spring of 1917 and then Ypres again, returning to the Somme in 1918. The battalion returned to Shrewsbury where it was disbanded in June 1919. More or less continuously in action, the 7th Battalion earned more battle honours than any other KSLI battalion but it also suffered more casualties, with over 1,048 men lost during the war.

7th Battalion KSLI Private 24079 George Geary from Madeley was killed in action on 28 March 1918 and is remembered on the Arras Memorial. His remains were never found.

The 8th Battalion was also raised in Shrewsbury during September 1914. Led by Lieutenant Colonel C.H. Sisted, it was sent to France in October 1915. The battalion was transferred to Macedonia, arriving in November 1915 where it remained throughout the war. Besides being employed in routine trench work on the defences of Salonika, where the men suffered badly from malaria, the battalion also took part in some severe fighting. In 1918 the battalion was in the final drive against the Bulgarian Army and, following the Armistice, it was sent into

Bulgaria. The 8th Battalion ended the war near Stavros and was eventually amalgamated with the 2nd Battalion KSLI in December 1918.

8th Battalion KSLI Private 16641 Samuel Knowles of Church Street, Oakengates was killed in action in Salonika on 25 April 1917 and is buried in the Karasouli Military Cemetery.

The 10th Battalion (Shropshire and Cheshire Yeomanry) was formed in March 1917 by amalgamating the troops of the Shropshire and Cheshire Yeomanry. The battalion served in the 74th or 'Broken Spur' Division, so called because it was made up from dismounted Yeomanry regiments. They were the only Shropshire unit to fight in Palestine against the Turks and in March 1918, during the battles of Tel Azur, Private Harold Whitfield was awarded the Victoria Cross. This became the only Victoria Cross to be awarded to a Shropshire Regiment during the First World War; in May 1918, the battalion then went on to France and eventually served on the Somme.

10th Battalion KSLI Private 231019 Private Thomas Harley of Lincoln Road, Wrockwardine Wood, died of pneumonia on 20 October 1918 and is buried in the Lapugnoy Military Cemetery. He had served with the Egyptian Expeditionary Force before going to France.

The 3rd and 9th Battalions were Reserve or Service Battalions who trained recruits and supplied reinforcements to the Regular Army.

Shropshire Yeomanry

The Shropshire Yeomanry mobilised on 4 August 1914 and, on a par with other cavalry regiments, consisted of three squadrons.

The 1st moved to East Anglia in September on coastal defence duties; whilst here a small motorcycle section was formed to act as messengers and dispatch riders. The unit eventually sailed for Egypt in November 1915 as an infantry regiment, although a few men did serve in the Imperial Camel Corps in the Sinai Desert.

During their time in Egypt the regiment was amalgamated and became the 10th Battalion KSLI.

The 2nd initially acted as a training and supply unit based at home. In July 1916, it was converted to a cyclist unit and served in Ireland before being disbanded in November 1918. Len Edwards recalls being drafted to this unit when he enlisted in 1915: 'we went to Northumberland … Newbiggin … It come as Cavalry wasn't needed and they took the horses off us and it was bikes, and I didn't care much about that.' As a result Len volunteered to go France.

The 3rd was formed in Shrewsbury in 1915 as a Reserve Regiment. This squadron was later based in Oswestry and finally disbanded in 1917, with the personnel being transferred to other regiments.

Royal Shropshire Horse Artillery

The Shropshire Royal Horse Artillery consisted of three units: Battery HQ, Shropshire Battery at Shrewsbury and the Welsh Border Mounted Ammunition Column based at Church Stretton. During the war they served as 'A' Battery 293rd Brigade Royal Field Artillery and 'A' Battery 158 Brigade, initially on coastal defence duties in East Anglia and, from 1917, on the Western Front. The men from the Artillery Column also served in France as a Royal Field Artillery Trench Mortar Unit.

Shropshire Soldiers

Not all those serving in the Shropshire battalions were Shropshire men and similarly not all Shropshire men served in Shropshire Regiments. Private 10753 Jack Butler, an ex-collier from Dawley, was with the 14th Division Mining Company attached to the New Zealand Tunnelling Company. These companies were involved in digging deep under no-man's-land and the German trenches, laying explosives in order to blow up the German lines.

Patriotism, comradeship and adventure were promoted in this recruitment drive for the Royal Marines. (Author's collection)

Mining and tunnelling for the British Expeditionary Force was 'not like working in the pits at home', wrote Jack – in some cases neither picks or shovels were used, instead old disused bayonets were employed. There were no tubs and rails to remove the soil, the earth was collected by hand, put into sandbags and carried out.

Shropshire lads also served at sea and in the air: Jack Hardman from Madeley was a Royal Marine aboard HMS *Castor* and had been involved in the Battle of Jutland, Air Mechanic Joseph Jones served initially in the Royal Navy before his transfer to the Naval Air Service and William Barnett from Broseley was a pilot with the infant RAF.

A number also served in colonial regiments: Sergeant Farr was with the Canadian Veterinary Unit at a hospital near Le Havre, whilst others served alongside Australian and New Zealand forces.

Life at the Front and in the Trenches

Correspondence and parcels from home were a lifeline for the soldiers serving at the trenches:

> ... words from home ... are sweet to every Tommy. It would do you good to see the rings of faces round the postman when letters are delivered & see the expressions on the faces of those who have one & those who have not, the contrast is great
>
> *Bert Oakes*

The majority of letters carried requests, especially for tobacco and cigarettes, though sometimes luxury items were asked for, such as motoring gloves lined with fur and fastened with a strap across the wrist:

> I want you to get me some tobacco and send to me, for I cannot get any out here, try and get me some 'Three Nuns' if possible, send me two tins as soon as possible for I haven't got a smoke, and then send regular every week, for as you know how I like my old pipe and I feel miserable without it.

… send me another writing pad out, like the one you gave me to bring back with me, for I have nearly finished that one and another thing you can send my pipes, the two wooden ones which I came away and forgot, in my hurry. I daresay you will find them either in my bedroom or somewhere on the mantelshelf in the kitchen …

An item that had recently become available was the fountain pen which was especially welcome:

Postcards were produced for servicemen to purchase and send home to their loved ones. (Ironbridge Gorge Museum Trust)

Dad … I want you to get me a fountain pen either a SWAN or WATERMAN, self-filler but not one with too thick a nib, for it would be very useful to me in my work at the present time, if you send it be sure and register it, and let me know how much it cost and I will refund the money by return, send a good one and get one of those pocket clips as well, do you think you could send a bottle of ink for it as well for such things are very dear out here.

Cecil 'Cis' Oakes

Private A.E. Corbett from Dawley wrote:

The fountain pen is the best present I have ever received since I left home, you can write when you go on guard without … taking a pen and ink with you.

The letters also provide information as to what friends and family sent out:

The pork pie … the Orderly Room Sergeant & myself enjoyed for supper with a nice drop of tea & rum.

I am thinking of you. at Portsmouth

... thank you both for the lovely box of plums, tobacco & sweets which arrived safe & sound on Saturday last. The fruit was lovely, such fine specimens, I can assure you they didn't last long.

Bert Oakes

Not all packages reached their destination, however. One soldier wrote to say that the parcel had been 'received in a very damaged state ... what contents were left I quite enjoyed but the very things I was looking forward to (tobacco & cigs) I am sorry to say they had walked for as you can guess Tommy likes to have a smoke of tobacco or cigs from dear old Blighty', whilst another wrote that 'the eggs I am sorry to say were rotten I had to throw them away for they were not fit to eat'.

The weather was always a topic and the conditions endured by the men were often reported:

Out here it is awful, 16 degrees of frost is not very nice to be living in ... this morning when I got up my tunic, which I had thrown over me before going to sleep, was covered with frost & this is in a house too. The water freezes as you wash ... & the bread is so hard with frost we have to thaw it before a knife will touch it.

Bert Oakes in France

Private W.E. Powell of the Shropshire Yeomanry camped on the banks of the River Nile and was, 'troubled with flies and mosquitoes ... I am so tormented I shall have to put on my mosquito net'.

And Private E. Baxter, 8th KSLI in Macedonia, was similarly affected: 'It is awfully hot out here and the flies are something dreadful.'

The soldiers' billets varied greatly depending on what they could find, from trenches to barns:

> To realize what it is like one has to actually be amongst it. You fancy digging a fair sized celery trench with caves on one side, just large enough for a man to get into & live, no matter what conditions the weather, & you have a miniature trench in modern warfare ... some of the dug outs are large & roomy – these are Company & Battalion Headquarters – but as wet as wells for the water soaks down & drips from the roof making a fearful quagmire under foot.

> ... we were sleeping in an old barn, and the cold was terrible, and it was simply swarmed with rats, well you could hear them going through a Bomb throwing course on the floor at nights, and over the top of us as well and I can assure you it made us feel very uncomfortable.

> I was given a rest down from the trenches this time, so at present am writing in a small tent sitting on a box with another for my table, a candle supported by 3 upright nails on a piece of wood ... & a petrol tin with holes punched in the sides forms my fire grate.

'I swung the prop to start the engine and the pilot said "Come on jump in Lane." I was thrilled, it was a wonderful opportunity, out over the Channel and the engine cut out; we made a forced landing and the pilot said "that was a bloody near one wasn't it Lane?" I did enjoy the flight though.'

William Lane, Air Mechanic Royal Flying Corp

And some billets were *much* better, as Private Jones from Lawley Farm discovered, having fought at the front and then started training new recruits just behind the lines:

> ... at a convent where there were 4 nuns and a number of old age pensioners, the cook and a gardener. We get on jolly well, in great demand for odd jobs repairing the walls, and roof and a hundred

other jobs. We also have use of their stove but with our coal we prepare the food but leave the cooking to them. Dinners are fine, meat, potatoes onions, cabbage or salad we hold services in the garden and a splendid brass band composed of men from different battalions play regularly.

When they were not in action there was a chance not only to wash, but to see something of the countryside:

This morning I went for a bath, not upstairs, but about 5½ miles away to a larger town. I cycled, & as the air was slightly frosty I enjoyed my journey very much. The bath, I was glad of, for I scarcely dare pull my coat off for fear of my shirt walking away, it was so much alive … now feel a new man again & much more comfortable.

[The French farmers] are making good use of the weather, working from daylight to dawn and Sunday as well for they are so anxious, poor things, to get it [the crops] in, some are under the range of shell fire, even to women & girls.

It is heart rendering [*sic*] to pass through what were once busy thriving towns & see the damage done & the derelict houses – many very large ones – blown almost all away. The people of England cannot realise what war is till they see it out here.

Whilst in the Far East, stationed in Hong Kong, one of the duties was to take German prisoners of war to Australia. Here they had an easy time and Private Corbett from Dawley wrote:

One would not know there was a war on – only they have a lot of Australian soldiers [at] home wounded. We had a fine time of it an old soldier took us for a ride around Sydney in his motor car when we stopped at different places the women made such a fuss of us.

Shropshire Men Awarded the Victoria Cross

Five men from Shropshire were awarded the Victoria Cross during the First World War:

Private Harold Edward Whitfield
Harold Whitfield of the 10th Battalion King's Shropshire Light Infantry (a farm worker from Pool Farm, Middleton, near Oswestry), enlisted in the Shropshire Yeomanry in 1908 and was eventually sent to the Middle East with his regiment. Harold was awarded the KSLI's first and only Victoria Cross of the First World War for his action at Burj-el-Lisaneh in May 1918:

> For most conspicuous bravery, initiative and disregarding personal safety ... [he] single handed charged and captured a Lewis gun which had been harassing his Company [at short range]. He turned the gun on the enemy and drove them back ... thereby completely restoring the whole situation in his part of the line.

Harold later organised and led an attack on the enemy's forward positions, driving them back and 'materially assisted in the defeat of the counter attack'.

When he returned home to Oswestry on leave in June 1918 he was welcomed as a local hero. A modest and unassuming man, Harold retired from the army in 1936 after twenty-eight years' service. He was killed on 19 December 1956, at the age of 70, as a result of a road accident.

Harold Whitfield's Victoria Cross and medal group, together with his rifle and bayonet, are now on display at the Regimental Museum in Shrewsbury Castle.

Lieutenant Thomas Orde Lawder Wilkinson
Thomas Wilkinson was born at The Lodge Farm, Dudmaston, near Bridgnorth and was educated at Wellington College. His family emigrated to Canada just before the war and Thomas enlisted in the Canadian Army but, on his arrival in

Lieutenant Thomas Orde Lawder Wilkinson VC of the 7th Battalion, the Loyal North Lancashire Regiment. The plaque is located in the churchyard of St Andrew, Quatt, the parish where Thomas was born. (Permission kindly given by the Martin Nicholson Cemetery Project)

Brass plaques of those awarded the VC have been inserted into the boardwalk surrounding the Lochnagar Crater. (Photograph by Brian Curran)

England, he was transferred as a Gunnery Officer with the rank of Temporary Lieutenant to the 7th Battalion Loyal North Lancashire Regiment.

He was posthumously awarded the Victoria Cross for his action on 5 July 1916 at La Boiselle when 'with great pluck and promptness he mounted a machine gun on top of a parapet and dispersed ... enemy bombers. He then made two most gallant attempts to bring in a wounded man ... but he was shot through the heart ... 40 yards in front of the Battalion's position.'

His body was never recovered and he is remembered on the Thiepval Memorial. His Victoria Cross is now displayed at the Imperial War Museum, London.

Able Seaman William Charles Williams

Memorial for Able Seaman William Charles Williams. (Author's collection)

William Williams was born in Stanton Lacy, though he was brought up in Chepstow. He joined the Boys Service section of the Royal Navy and progressed through the ranks; in 1901 he was aboard HMS *Terrible* in China during the Boxer Rebellion.

At the outbreak of war he rejoined the Royal Navy and, in 1915, was serving on the SS *River Clyde* assisting in the landings at Gallipoli. Although under heavy fire, William stood chest-deep in water holding on to a rope for over an hour until dangerously wounded. Sadly he was killed by a shell before he could be rescued and was buried at sea. Able Seaman Williams was posthumously awarded the Victoria Cross for valour on 25 April 1915 for his action.

William's medals – which along with the Victoria Cross include the Queen's South Africa Medal (1899–1902), with two clasps for Tugela Heights and the Relief of Ladysmith; the China War Medal (1900); the 1914–15 Star, British War Medal and the Victory Medal – are now part of the Ashcroft Collection and on display in the Imperial War Museum.

A war memorial commemorating William's bravery is located in Beaufort Square, Chepstow. A plaque on the gun states:

> This gun, taken from a captured German submarine, was presented by His Majesty King George the Fifth to the town of Chepstow in recognition of the award of the Victoria Cross to Able Seaman Charles Williams R.F.R. of this town. During the landing from the 'River Clyde' at V. Beach, Seddul Bahr, he assisted in replacing in position the lighters forming the bridge to the shore and which had broken adrift, holding on to a line in the water for over an hour until killed.

Major Charles Allix Lavington Yate

Charles Yate, known from his initials as 'Cal', was born in Germany in 1872. However, he was brought up in Madeley where his father, the Revd George Yate, served as vicar for over fifty years. Major Yate of the King's Own Yorkshire Light Infantry (KOYLI) had served in the South African War and, on his return to Madeley station, local miners pulled his carriage through the streets to his home.

A number of men were recalled from the army to work on munitions. Private Holbrook was one of thirty-two men who were returned to the army once more: '[I am] back on my old job ... on the machine-gun and I shan't be long before I'm out again for the third time.'

Private A. Holbrook, 3rd KSLI

CHRISTMAS AT THE FRONT

Christmas is a particularly difficult time for communities at war, with family members and friends noticeably absent from any festive celebrations. Those at home, as the *Dawley News* reported, 'have very little heart to be merry'. Nonetheless, during the First World War every family and community organisation attempted to send out Christmas parcels to the men overseas. Hadley sent fifteen parcels containing a scarf, tobacco, chocolate, a mug, letters, a book and a Christmas card.

Most seem to have sent out some type of festive food: 'I shouldn't have known it was Christmas Day if it hadn't been for the plum pudding & mince pies which dear mother sent out to me,' wrote Cis Oakes.

There were also Christmas truces at the front line and Gunner Tart, 112 Battery, Royal Field Artillery wrote of Christmas Day:

A German shouted 'give us a fag & we'll give you some beer' some of the Germans came halfway across the British trenches and were met by our fellows. We had a pair of socks each from [the] Queen, a Xmas card from the King, a pipe and tobacco from Princess Mary.

But most longed for peace and to be home with their families:

Give my best love to all members of the family & wish them the same Good Old Wish & God willing may we never spend Christmas under such circumstances again. As I write – today Christmas Eve – you are talking around a good fire, as it should be, whilst I, well, never mind. I am only one of thousands, so roll on Peace & let we chaps get back to wives & those we love so dear. I hope I shall never see another Xmas under the same conditions as today. Your loving son Bert.

Sadly Bert Oakes was killed in action on 30 September 1917. He is buried in the Brandhoek New Military Cemetery.

Christmas cards sent from the front made of silk embroidered with coloured silks. The motto reads, 'Am cheery how's yourself' and this silk flap folds back to reveal the words 'from your loving son'. (Ironbridge Gorge Museum Trust)

A regimental Christmas card sent from France by Bert Oaks to his parents. It shows a British soldier from the Peninsular Wars (1807–14) encouraging the First World War British 'Tommy' to 'Carry On'. Inscribed on the base of the column on the right-hand side is a list of battles, with more recent ones added underneath. (Author's collection)

A 'Thinking of You' postcard. Designs in this theme were produced in their thousands for the servicemen to send home to their sweethearts. (Ironbridge Gorge Museum Trust)

He served in Japan and was awarded the Russo-Japanese War Medal and the Japanese Order of the Sacred Treasure by the emperor. He went on to work at the War Office but, on the outbreak of war, chose to serve in the army and rejoined the KOYLI.

On 24 August 1914, at Le Cateau, 'when all other officers were killed or wounded and all ammunition exhausted he led his 19 survivors against the enemy in a charge in which he was severely wounded and picked up by the enemy'. Major Yate died on 20 September 1914 as a prisoner of war in Germany and was posthumously awarded the Victoria Cross. His medals are on display at the KOYLI Regimental Museum in Pontefract.

Brigadier-General John Vaughan Campbell

John Campbell was born on 31 October 1876 in London but, prior to the war, was living at Broom Hall, Oswestry where he was Master of the local Tanat Side Hunt.

During the Battle of the Somme, 15 September 1916, John Campbell served as commanding officer of the 3rd Coldstream Guards, taking personal command of the third wave of his battalion after the first two lines were decimated by machine gun and rifle fire. He led his men to capture the enemy machine guns and, on 15 September 1916, he was awarded the Victoria Cross for his gallantry and initiative in ensuring that these vital tactical objectives were taken. During the war he earned the nickname of the 'Tally-ho' VC as he used the sound of a huntsman's horn to rally his men.

Brigadier-General John Vaughan Campbell VC, CMG (Companion (of the Order of) St Michael and St George), DSO, died on 21 May 1944 at his home Benwell House, near Stroud. There is a memorial plaque in Cawdor parish church near Nairn, Scotland and his medals are on display in the Coldstream Guards Museum.

5

HOME FIRES BURNING

Despite, or perhaps in spite of, the war, most communities throughout Great Britain tried to continue as they had done before August 1914. In July 1915 'The all British Institution, Lord John Sanger's Royal Circus and Menagerie' visited a number of towns; it included the 'Russian Cossack Display' as well as sea lions, elephants, acrobats and clowns. Carnivals, parades and every kind of social gathering were still arranged but now all included fund-raising for the war effort.

This postcard is dated 5 February 1917. The bridge in the background is the Albert Edward railway bridge and the building on the right is the Ironbridge Rowing Clubhouse. This was the first time in twenty-five years that the river had frozen over. Charley Bagley is on the motorbike with passengers Billy and Beattie Brown, and it was also reported that 'there were many skaters'. (Author's collection)

DAWLEY NEWS

The *Dawley News* was a magazine-style publication produced by the brotherhood and sisterhood of the Dawley Baptist church. It was sold for 1*d* at their Tuesday meetings on the understanding that, once read, it would be sent to a Dawley man on military service. It began in the autumn of 1915 and was made up of about eight handwritten pages that were then duplicated on a Cyclostyle machine (a sort of copier); a number of people helped in its production but the central figure was probably the pastor, Arthur Lester.

The content was made up of local news and gossip, together with cartoons and sketches, but most importantly contained news from the men themselves. Articles, news and letters were sent from all corners of the world: from serving soldiers on the Western Front, from those in both the Middle and Far East, from ships, from prisoners of war and those in hospitals both at home and abroad. There was a constant plea from 'the editors' for soldiers to write and an open invitation when they were on leave to visit the chapel meetings.

The cost of producing the newspaper was financed from the sales at meetings, with the balance then used to send copies to serving men; all welcomed its arrival, Private P. Brown from 'somewhere East' wrote to ask that the paper continue being sent as 'a word from home acts like a tonic'.

As the war progressed, local casualties were reported together with requests from family for news about those missing. In 1916 a War Information Bureau was set up by Mr Preece to co-ordinate inquiries, believing that through direct personal enquires information could be obtained more quickly. The newspaper also asked, on behalf of bereaved families, for photographs of the graves of those buried abroad.

Front page cover of the Weekly Report *(later renamed the* Dawley News*) dated 20 June 1916. (Kindly loaned by Mr Toby Neal)*

Cartoon from the Dawley News *of the ladies collecting the eggs, the hen on the car is saying 'We're all doing our bit!'*

Fund-raising and Collecting

Collecting goods of various kinds and raising money seems to have taken over most communities throughout the war. Nationally the Prince of Wales Fund and regular 'War Weapons Weeks' all raised the profile of fund-raising for the war effort. Towns arranged these 'War Weapons Weeks' to encourage investments in National War Bonds and War Savings Certificates; an added inducement from the War Office was the consent to name an aeroplane after the locality.

Outside the Anstice Working Men's Club, in Park Avenue, Madeley, this image shows a decorated float taking part in the carnival of 1917. A number of children and young ladies are dressed as nurses with a young man as a patient in the bed; the sign calls for donations 'In Aid of the War Fund'. (Madeley Town Council Archive)

Numerous committees were set up in every town in order to support the various causes. Within days of the outbreak of war, Hadley Parish Council, like hundreds of other communities in Shropshire, called a meeting in order to set up a 'relief or distress fund' for dependents of serving men. Funds were also organised for Belgian refugees, hospitals, the Red Cross, prisoners of war, wounded soldiers and 'Comfort Funds' for sending goods to serving men. The Dawley Baptist community recorded that, in December 1916, they had dispatched 106 different parcels to Dawley men; the goods in each parcel cost on average between 5s and 6s, plus 1s per parcel for carriage.

Traditional social events, such as concerts and whist drives, now became geared to raising funds, while house-to-house collections and sales of work brought in extra money for the cause. A sale of donated goods in aid of the Red Cross was held in Dawley Market Hall and amongst the gifts were supplies of coal, swedes and firewood together with livestock, two pigs, a calf and a sheep (which escaped and 'ran amok among the people').

The established Sewing and Knitting Guilds turned to producing scarves or mufflers, socks, gloves and helmets for soldiers, as well as things to sell. Red Cross workrooms were set up throughout Shropshire where volunteers supplied the county hospitals with bandages, pads, splints, etc.

Employees of numerous companies contributed to relief funds to aid families of workmates who were serving, with the miners of the Madeley Wood Colliery contributing 6*d* per week for a man and 3*d* for a boy, whilst those earning over £2 per week contributed 1*s*. At Audley Engineering it was reported that twenty-six staff, out of fifty volunteers, had agreed to pay weekly between 5*s* and 10*s* to a relief fund in aid of those families whose employees were serving.

Postcard of French soldiers amongst the ruins of the marketplace in Verdun. A number of 'Battlefield' images were taken and postcards were produced to help raise funds. (Ironbridge Gorge Museum Trust)

Patriotic sale at Clun, 8 September 1915. The townsfolk of Clun are gathered round on what appears to be a hot sunny day, in order to support the sale of goods in aid of the war, possibly to be auctioned by the vicar, standing right. (Kindly loaned by Ray Farlow)

War-related items were also displayed in order to raise money and a German gun, captured at Loos by the 7th Division on 25 September 1915, was paraded in various towns throughout the summer of 1916 with the money going to wounded British soldiers.

Books and magazines were collected and sent, not just to those serving abroad, but also to those National Reserve soldiers who were on duty in Britain but away from home. With a similar aim in mind, there was also a plea for books to stock a library at the Park Hall Camp which would be managed by the Young Men's Christian Association (YMCA).

As both food rationing and patients increased many hospitals struggled to cope, causing their managers to look to local people for help and for donations of goods. In a letter to the Dawley Baptist church, the secretary of the VAD hospital at Wellington College stated that the grant 'was inadequate to meet their outgoings "so they were dependent on other help", any donations of vegetables, fruit, eggs and rabbits all helped to ease the food bills.'

The Trench Lion. Part of a bicycle fancy dress parade, with 'The Catch of the Season' being the Kaiser at the front line! (Kindly loaned by Ray Farlow)

A war depot at Ludlow. The group of ladies are producing items of medical supplies, both for the local hospitals and to be sent abroad. (Kindly loaned by Ray Farlow)

During 1915 a National Egg Collection was instigated, both for local hospitals and to send to the front. In the spring of that year, Mrs Dugdale and Mrs Swire started an egg collection in Shrewsbury for the Royal Shropshire Infirmary and other hospitals caring for wounded soldiers. A number of communities, and especially schools, organised similar collections. Oliver Rickers from Newdale remembered that they 'used to take eggs into school to be sent to the troops in hospital, we put our names on the eggs and sometimes got a message back'.

Food

An advert for Egg Week. (Wellington Journal and Shrewsbury News)

After the declaration of war there had been an initial period of panic buying though most grocers and provision dealers appeared to have regulated sales themselves. As a mainly rural county, most

SPECIAL EGG WEEK FOR OUR WOUNDED SOLDIERS.

URGENT REQUEST FOR 1,000,000 EGGS (ONE MILLION) DURING THE WEEK COMMENCING AUGUST 16.
Patron—HER MAJESTY QUEEN ALEXANDRA.
The following SCOUTS, &c.. will assist in the Collection for Wellington and District :—
1st WELLINGTON, Scoutmaster, Mr. T. Tranter.
2nd   Ditto   Ditto   Mr. Geo. Riley.
1st HADLEY   Ditto   Mr. A. McIntyre.
WELLINGTON BOYS' LIFE BRIGADE, Captain Hammond.
    Eggs from any source gratefully received.
Depot for receiving and forwarding in Wellington district—

J. L.   E. T. Morgan

CHURCH STREET.

Shropshire families had access to dairy products, home-grown vegetables, eggs and chickens, with many even keeping a pig. However, as the war progressed the government began to intervene, issuing controlled prices and a voluntary rationing of bread, meat and sugar. By November 1917, Sir Arthur Yapp, Director of Food Economy, warned that 'the strictest economy should be practiced in the use of staple foods', a list of recommended weekly rations was published with all cereals and fats now added to the list. A more extensive use of fresh vegetables and fruit was encouraged, especially potatoes which were not rationed.

During 1916 the Cultivation of Lands Order was passed and Shrewsbury's Improvement Committee inspected every 'garden capable of producing food crops' to ensure it was brought into cultivation. They 'procured' 298 allotments of around 300 square yards and these were leased for a rental of 7s 6d per year, providing that three-quarters of the land was planted with potatoes.

By 1917 the shortage of cereals, especially wheat for bread, was extremely serious and flour for home cooking was so poor

This photograph, taken on 9 June 1917 outside the old markets in Madeley (now Jubilee House, the Madeley Town Council Offices), shows children with baskets and sacks queuing to buy potatoes from Mr Rock, a farmer from nearby Kemberton. (Madeley Town Council Archives)

Mr Rock of Kemberton "selling potatoes in Madeley", June 9

Sugar Distribution under the Government Scheme.

Instructions to Householders.

1st.—All Customers must apply to the Local Post Office for Sugar Application Forms on or before September 29th.

2nd.—When you receive these forms return without a stamp to the Local Food Control Office with J. C. LLOYD'S name as your Grocer not later than October 6th.

3rd.—Do not be misled by grocers asking you to sign papers in their establishment registering with them as their Grocers as it is unofficial.

Any further particulars apply

LLOYD'S STORES,

Shifnal, Wellington, Newport, Albrighton.

This notice in the local newspaper dates from September 1917, but from 1916 the newspapers printed many similar notices regarding the rationing of food, especially those which were imported. (Wellington Journal and Shrewsbury News)

that Elizabeth Davies remembered her grandmother stopped baking. Around this time, the Salop War Agricultural Executive Committee reported that food shortages were 'enormous and menacing' and actively encouraged the replacement of bread with potatoes in the diet (since potatoes, unlike wheat, were in good supply). At the Maypole in Shrewsbury, the queues 'stretched right around the Square and sometimes down Gullet Passage … all for 2ozs of margarine' and another county resident recalled being sent with a basin to buy 'lovely, brown dripping with jelly' for 2d as they didn't get enough meat to make their own.

Sugar was amongst the first commodities to be 'controlled' and led the government to encourage farmers to cultivate sugar-beet. Post-war, a number of sugar-beet factories were constructed, including one at Allscott in 1927, between Admaston and Shrewsbury. The scarcity of sugar meant that many people gave it up in tea in order to make jam, although if fruit was grown an extra allowance was available. Hunting down required foodstuffs became part of the daily routine and whenever a new supply arrived in store the news would quickly spread and children were sent after school or even allowed time off to queue.

Education

At this time most children attended just one elementary school from the age 4 or 5 until they left at 14 years to go to work; although, Arthur Lewis recalled that during the war, 'if you got a job in a war factory you could leave at 13½'. If parents could afford it, or if pupils excelled and obtained a scholarship, then secondary and further education would be open to them. Generally elementary schools were mixed and secondary school were single sex. Access to a university education was also possible but rare.

Girls sitting exams at the private Hiatt School in Wellington would remain in their classrooms until 7.00 p.m. instead of taking work home as fuel and light were in short supply. Meanwhile, those taking the Senior Oxford Examination in Shrewsbury would stay overnight all week as trains were unreliable.

Olive Rickers said that, at Newdale School, they did a lot of knitting for soldiers, making socks, scarves and helmets. 'One girl would do one sock and me another we put our names on them and the lads from the trenches used to write back we were so proud when we got letters back.' Some teachers took the opportunity to illustrate the development of the war; 'our teacher had two maps and lots of wool, one in red and one in yellow, one for our soldiers and one for the enemy, when we had news he would move the wool, saying we had been driven back or gained some land'.

The shortage of paper meant a return to slates, which some children thought were 'lovely to write on, make a mistake and a little drop of spit would rub it out'. Newspapers and magazines also found supplies difficult and began to use both cheaper paper and reduce the number of pages.

Nearly every town made facilities available for servicemen that were waiting for onward transportation (either home on leave or back to the front) and in Wellington a military canteen was opened for the use of soldiers and sailors. The premises, in Crown Street, were kindly lent by Mr John Kynaston and had a reading room with writing materials, as well as the usual refreshment facilities.

A large number of these organisations and facilities were managed by ladies, who were generally the wives and daughters of local business or professional men. Most ladies worked within their own locality or at least within the county, but occasionally someone of exception stepped forward. One such was Mrs Katherine Harley.

Mrs Katherine Harley

This brass plaque to Mrs Katherine Harley is located inside Parade Shopping Centre in Shrewsbury; this building had once been the Royal Salop Infirmary Hospital where she worked as a nurse. (Author's collection)

Described as 'an extraordinary woman from an extraordinary family', Katherine 'Katie' Harley lived at Condover House, Condover and was the widow of Colonel George Ernest Harley and the sister to both Field Marshall Sir John French and the notable suffragette Charlotte Despard. Katherine too was an early member of the Women's Suffrage Movement; although not as militant as her sister, she was known to be headstrong, impatient and not very easy to work with.

As a trained nurse she worked at the Royal Shrewsbury Infirmary and was one of the first women to offer her services for the war effort, taking a position as a member of

the Scottish Women's Hospitals Committee. Under the auspices of this committee, the first women's medical unit (which included Katherine Harley) was in France by December 1914 and, in the following spring, a group of British nurses (which again included Katie) went to Serbia in order to establish medical facilities there.

Working under French command, Katherine was in charge of the medical unit that the *Wellington Journal* reported 'consisted entirely of women surgeons, women physicians, and women physicists for the X-rays, women nurses, orderlies and chauffeurs'. In April 1916, Katherine Harley was presented with the Croix de Guerre for her 'splendid service in connection with her Red Cross work in both France and Serbia'.

Almost a year later, on Wednesday, 7 March 1917, Katherine Harley was killed at Monastir. Although exact details of her death are confused, it seems that she was probably hit by shellfire. She was buried with full military honours in the Salonika (Lembit Road) Military Cemetery, Thessalonika, Greece, where the grave bears a private memorial which towers above all the others in the cemetery. Erected in 1917 by the Serbian Army, this memorial is inscribed in two languages and reads: 'The generous English lady and great benefactress of the Serbian people, Madame Harley a great lady. On your tomb instead of flowers the gratitude of the Serbs shall blossom there for your wonderful acts. Your name shall be known from generation to generation.'

Following Katherine's death, a memorial fund was raised in her honour, with part of the money being used to endow a cot in the Royal Shrewsbury Infirmary and the remainder invested with the income used to fund a nursing medal. The Katherine M. Harley Memorial Medals for Efficiency were awarded annually to two outstanding nurses on completion of their training and the medal was still being awarded up to 1969.

MORE UNUSUAL FUND-RAISING SCHEMES
Mrs R.S. Richards of Whittington organised a collection for a gramophone and records to be sent to the engineering staff aboard HMS *Greyhound*.

A street collection arranged by the Shrewsbury Neapolitan Organ-Grinders raised £25 for the benefit of wounded soldiers in local hospitals.

Katherine Harley is also commemorated with a memorial at the parish church of St Mary the Virgin, Shrewsbury and in Condover parish church, while in the village Harley Road is named in her memory.

Although working overseas, Mrs Harley continued to encourage Shropshire ladies in their fund-raising and volunteer work, leading the way by raising the money for a military motor canteen to serve the soldiers at the front. Mrs Luard, wife of Lieutenant Colonel Luard, commanding officer of the 1st Battalion KSLI, was instrumental in the organisation of a prisoner-of-war fund.

Shropshire Prisoners of War

Allied soldiers were taken as prisoners of war from the first battles of the conflict and of course this included Shropshire men. Amongst the first were two Madeley men: Victoria Cross recipient Major Yate and Private 7973 Harry Brown of the 2nd Battalion Duke of Westminster's (West Riding) Regiment. Sadly both of these men died as prisoners of war, Major Yate on 20 September 1914 and Private Brown on 26 January 1915. They are buried in the Berlin South-Western Cemetery.

As information regarding prisoners of war trickled home through the War Office or the International Red Cross, so the local newspapers printed the details of those who had been captured. In June 1915, Mrs Luard suggested the setting up of a prisoner-of-war fund. By 1917 the King's Shropshire Light Infantry Prisoner of War Fund was organised, with a staff of volunteers who worked to ensure that three parcels were sent to each man every two weeks. The number of prisoners increased, especially through 1918, so that by the end of the war over 900 men were receiving parcels. 'All the parcels from you rank among the best. Without a single exception they have all arrived here in most perfect condition,' wrote one of the men.

A number of towns and villages also set up their own fund in order to assist local men who were prisoners. The Brotherhood and Sisterhood of the Dawley Baptist church was one such organisation, and they also offered help to the families on what and how to send correspondence. The post office, they stated, advise the sending of postcards for correspondence or to write only two pages, leave the envelope unsealed and to include only private or family information. A letter sent to Stoker Rowe in Holland on notepaper that was 'emblazoned' with the Union Jack was returned by the censor!

> **WAR SAVINGS CERTIFICATES**
> 'The Government Plan Explained. The certificates cost 15/6d, for which you will get £1 in 5 years' time; a War Savings Card can also be obtained at the post office for 6d stamps, once the 31 spaces are filled then it can be exchanged for a certificate.'

The volunteers at the Baptist Chapel raised funds to send parcels to the prisoners. Bugler E. Round of the Welsh Fusiliers, originally from Meadow Road, Dawley, was a prisoner in an English Camp in Hanover, Germany and they sent him 'three loaves a week … to help keep him alive'. Another parcel, containing butter, cheese and cooked bacon, was sent sometime later and Bugler Round wrote to say that the food arrived in good condition and was 'very much appreciated'.

In the same way that German prisoners of war were made to work in Britain, so the prisoners of war in Germany were utilised to help out where necessary. In July 1916, a letter from Bugler Round noted that he was working on a farm with nine other English prisoners. The weather and the surroundings were both fine and that he 'liked it very well, it is better than being in camp'.

By February 1915, negotiations instigated by the American ambassador to Berlin (with assistance from the International Red Cross) enabled wounded and sick prisoners from both sides to be transferred to Switzerland, a neutral country, on the grounds of ill health. Private 10754 Jim Alford, of the 5th KSLI and originally from Heath Hill, near Dawley, was wounded prior to being taken prisoner, 'with a good many others' and wrote in April 1916 to say, 'We've been treated very well by the German hospital men.' He arrived at a camp in Giessen, Germany but, in August 1916, he was amongst around 700 sent to Switzerland: 'I can't describe the reception we got, people waving, jumping about and handing us cigarettes.'

The mountains and lakes, especially after the camp, were 'simply lovely'; he was billeted at Manor Farm, Interlaken with an English lady and 'I can tell you we have just had our first dinner and it was jolly fine'.

Wives and families were able to visit the soldiers in Switzerland and, under the direction of the Red Cross, left London every few weeks. Jim Alford reported seeing them but noted that it was a very long way to travel for such a short time, especially since crossing the Channel was 'the very worst'. One other shortcoming was that free letters were restricted in Switzerland and stamps had to be purchased at 2½d each. As a result, Private Alford said people at home would now receive fewer letters from him.

Holland was also a neutral country and a number of British naval internees stayed there including Stoker 6097 George Rowe, a Royal Naval Reserve who was interned at Groningen. It was probable that he was at Antwerp, Belgium in October 1914 when the naval forces were overwhelmed by German infantry and naval officers led their men to Holland, hoping to avoid imprisonment in Germany. Nevertheless, George Rowe wrote that Holland was 'not a very bright place'.

Belgian Refugees

By the middle of September 1914, almost 500 Belgian refugees were arriving in London every day. As a result, War Refugee Committees began to be set up all over the country in order to raise funds to assist these families and to offer homes and shelter where necessary. Shropshire was no exception and from October 1914 the Shropshire Education Committee consented to free school places in secondary schools for all Belgian refugees.

Ken Corbett of Wellington recalled that the Shepherd family of No. 1 Park Street was amongst the first to offer their home. He states that 'A large crowd lined Station Road to see them arrive and they were welcomed by Mr Morgan, a local draper and Chairman of the Reception committee'. In Shrewsbury, a spacious building known as the old Armoury was converted into apartments and both goods and services were given or loaned by volunteers and local tradesmen.

Two Belgian refugee families settled in the Dawley area: the Deleuses and the Mortiers. Mr and Mrs Deleus, along with their five children, moved to Horsehay where Mr Deleus had obtained employment at the Horsehay Works. The local press reported that Mr Deleus had been 'badged' (i.e. awarded a badge in recognition of the war work he was undertaking) so that he would not be called up for military service. Meanwhile, Mr and Mrs Mortier, with their four children, arrived in Lawley Bank about October 1914. Around two years later, Mr Mortier was offered a place at the Cadbury's cocoa factory in Bourneville where he worked in the packing department alongside other Belgian refugees. The family moved to Sparkbrook and the community of Dawley Baptist church offered assistance in the transportation of their belongings.

Outings and Excursions

Regular local day trips were continued whenever possible. In July 1916, Mrs Patchett of the Hadley Wesleyan Mothers' Meeting organised a trip to Haughmond Hill for lunch and on to Shrewsbury, tea, shopping and home. The following day, not to be outdone the Church Mothers' Meeting Society, a group led by the vicar, Mrs Tranter and Mrs Marshall, went to Wolverhampton; the trip included a picnic, tea and shopping.

Companies also ensured their employees' planned excursions went ahead and the Engineering Department of the Horsehay Company went on their annual excursion to Condover Lodge where they had tea and fished! Capewell Horse Nail Works men went to Bridgnorth and, despite the showery

---

NATIONAL EGG COLLECTION
The response to the appeal for eggs produced the following:

Date – eggs collected
1915 – 70, 927
1916 – 67, 110
1917 – 62, 789
1918 – 53, 685

All the hospitals welcomed this addition to the diet of the patients.

The Forest Glen Refreshment Pavilion at its original location at the foot of the Wrekin; the building was removed and rebuilt at the Ironbridge Gorge Museum's Victorian Town at Blists Hill. (Ironbridge Gorge Museum Trust)

weather, they had a 'real good time' including a trip on the river, while the workforce of Messrs A.J. Stevens Engineering Company of Wolverhampton visited the Wrekin and was provided with tea at the Forest Glen by Mr and Mrs Pointon.

Industry

Most industrial concerns sought to turn their manufacture to the war effort in some form or another but a shortage of labour, together with the pressure to produce, could result in accidents and injuries. Absence from work became a criminal offence and an employee of Blackley's government-controlled brickworks in Hadley was ordered to pay 15s as a machine had been rendered idle by his absence.

Fire could be a big problem as there was no overall national fire service and instead each local council was responsible for its area. On 20 December 1916 the tannery and leather warehouses of James Cock & Co. in Shrewsbury, one of the biggest establishments of its kind in the Midlands, suffered a huge fire. The glare, explosions and crackling timbers caused the townsfolk to fear a Zeppelin attack, whilst the final cost of the damages was reported to be around £50,000.

Seven miners from the Woodhouse Colliery in St Georges nearly lost their lives in July 1916 whilst descending the shaft at the start of their day shift. The accident occurred between 5–6 a.m. when the cage in which they were travelling suddenly fell rapidly nearly to the bottom, then quickly rose a few yards before becoming stuck. Three of the occupants were thrown out as the gate of the cage opened but the others remained imprisoned for over four hours. At the surface the winding gear had smashed portions of the engine house, but thankfully, the driver was unscathed.

Medical assistance was immediately called for and Drs McCarthy and Pearson arrived together with the various colliery managers. The two doctors went down another shaft with a group of rescue workers and had to walk 2 miles underground to reach the injured men. Those thrown from the cage were stretchered out and removed to the Lilleshall Company's hospital in St Georges. Eventually, after some considerably time, the cage was lowered and the remaining four men were treated before being taken to the surface.

Woodhouse Colliery, St Georges, site of the accident in July 1916 when seven men nearly lost their lives. (Ironbridge Gorge Museum Trust)

MARKET DRAYTON SOLDIERS CIGARETTE AND TOBACCO FUND
In August 1916, collecting boxes were placed around the town (mainly in public houses and hotels) and by December of that year some 11,417 cigarettes, 72 ounces of tobacco, forty-one dozen boxes of matches and thirteen pipes had been sent out to servicemen.

Those involved were: William Overton from New Street; James Norton, Granville Street; Harry Groom, Ketley (all thrown from the cage); Harry Williams, West Street (a crushed foot and fractured thigh); John Simpson, Snedshill (fractured skull); Thomas Radcliffe, The Nabb; and Isaiah Williams, Snowhill.

As men were discharged from the services through injury or illness (generally described as 'no longer physically fit for war service'), a number were able to return to work in some capacity. If their disability was not obvious, however, then some were seen as 'shirkers' or conscientious objectors and suffered abuse. Fred Withington was discharged in November 1917 and received a pension of 22s a week, but he found it necessary to contact the War Office requesting his discharge badge. This would then be a visible sign to the general public that he had served in the war; a badge was subsequently sent with instructions that it was to be worn on the right breast or lapel and never on a naval or military uniform.

Conscientious Objectors and Pacifists

There were very few contemporary reports in Shropshire regarding either conscientious objectors or pacifists and those that did were usually as a result of a court case. In 1916 a conscientious objector from Yeovil avoided imprisonment by being accepted for work at a market garden in Wellington. The judge stressed that this was only acceptable provided the produce from the garden was for 'general consumption and not luxuries'.

A more disturbing incident was that of 27-year-old Arthur Horton from Manchester, who was incarcerated in Shrewsbury prison for his beliefs. In January 1918, he died there of bronchial pneumonia and heart failure and an inquest was held at

conscientious OBJECTION
1916
1919

Be faithful to that ancient testimony borne by us ever since we were a people against bearing arms + fighting.

Wandsworth 22.IV.18

Alternative Service hospital orderly agricultural worker forester

which Arthur's father stated that his son had complained of the depravation suffered by conscientious objectors in the prison. However, the jury, having seen the prison diet and considered it 'good', returned a verdict of 'natural causes'.

In more recent times, evidence has come to light of a camp for conscientious objectors situated at Ditton Priors where the men worked at the Brown Clee Quarry. A wooden hut sited in the village was burnt down during the night of 16 June 1918, apparently no one was injured but some felt that it was a deliberate act.

In 1917 two woman from Manchester and one from Whitchurch were accused of distributing pacifist related leaflets at Prees Heath Military Camp in order to 'disaffect those soldiers stationed there'. All three were imprisoned.

This is a panel from the Quaker Tapestry, an international project exploring Quaker history. The panel shows a Quaker before a tribunal and being shown the 'white feather' by a group of women, a prison cell where a number of conscientious objectors were incarcerated and the alternative war services that many took part in – hospital work (both home and overseas) and agricultural work. (Author's collection)

6

COMING HOME

The posting of a central news wire or telegram at the *Shrewsbury Chronicle* newspaper offices was the first intimation that the county had of the cessation of hostilities. As the news spread the town square began to fill up and boys from Shrewsbury School arrived with bugles and drums which 'intensified the enthusiasm'. In the evening, Shrewsbury streets were 'ablaze with fireworks', Canadian and American troops came in from the surrounding camps and joined in the celebrations 'Wild-West' style.

Ken Corbett of Wellington, a schoolboy at the time, recalled in his book that, 'school finished for the day at 11.00 and I went down the town with my mother and sister. Flags and bunting had appeared … as if by magic.' Mr J.W. Clift, chairman of the Urban Council, spoke to the crowd from the balcony of the Wrekin Hotel in Wellington's Market Square. The national anthem was sung, accompanied by Mr Charles Ralph who played a cornet, but it was reported that the jubilation of the event was subdued as people remembered the 'sorrowful memories of what victory had cost'.

Len Edwards was home on leave when the Armistice was signed: 'We was in Broseley and all the bells blowed [were rung], we went to the Post Office and an old road man said "You'll be alright now you wonna have to go back." We had to go back of course.'

The news took longer to reach the men at the front line, William Newill of the 1st Battalion KSLI remembered, 'We were in the firing line when the Armistice was signed.

It was 10 o'clock before we knew it was to be signed at eleven, and I think all hell was let loose in that last hour, and I'm sure they went over time.'

Industry

On hearing that the war had ended, Maisie Jennings recalled that Mr Rickus, the works manager at Sankey's, shouted at the top of his voice: 'Lads it's all over, we've won the war.' The workforce immediately downed tools, all except those in the panel shop who continued to bang out the news on the panels, 'Of course no more work [was done] that day' said Maisie.

At the Horsehay Works the hooter sounded and the workmen were assembled in the yard where Mr Simpson, the managing director, addressed the employees, stating that there would be a half day holiday. He added that some 530 employees would receive a £1 War Savings Certificate and the apprentices would receive a 15s Savings Certificate as a thanksgiving. George White said, 'I couldn't wait to receive mine, I knew what I would do with it, I went straight to the Post Office and cashed it and

A decorated float taking part in the 1917 Madeley Carnival, the picture is taken outside the Anstice Working Men's Club, in Park Avenue. The munition girls are probably from the Court Works Ltd and the posters state 'Doing Our Bit Till The Boys Come Home', so it is clear that they are aware that their employment is just 'for the duration'. (Madeley Town Council Archive)

DISASTROUS FIRE AT PARK HALL, OSWESTRY
The historic Elizabethan mansion, together with a fine art collection, was entirely destroyed by the fire which started just before midnight on Boxing Day 1918. During the war the grounds had been a training camp for a number of regiments and the house had been the staff headquarters at the military camp.

bought my first pair of football boots they cost me 14/11 with 1*d* change'.

True to their word, many works did keep the jobs open for those men who had been away during the war, but this was often at the expense of others. Arthur Bland went straight to the Horsehay Works from school and was later taken on as an apprentice template-maker. He remembered, 'We got a wonderful time during the war, had lads working for us' but when the 'chaps all came back … they were promised their jobs back … We had to step down and work for them.' This did not suit many of the nearly qualified apprentices and a number, including Arthur, left and 'went to the Sentinel' (a works in Shrewsbury).

Despite the work carried out by the women during the war, once the men began to return the majority left, either returning to the home or to domestic-related employment. Ethel Hudson's mother, who had been employed at Maws working on mosaics, did not continue after the war and Winifred Egan, who had worked at Coalbrookdale, went to be a house parlourmaid.

Coming Home

Although the Armistice was signed on 11 November 1918, the official ending of hostilities between Germany and the Allied Powers was the signing of the Treaty of Versailles on 28 June 1919. As a consequence, the first of the servicemen did not begin to return home until the first months of that year. Private Thomas Frederick Littler, who had served with the Cheshire Regiment, arrived at Prees (now a demobilisation centre) at 3.00 a.m. on 7 February 1919. He came in by train, handed in his kit and rifle, collected his papers, had breakfast and left for home by an 11.00 a.m. train.

However, not all soldiers had the same experiences, William Newill reported that:

> We went to Germany instead of coming home and we had Christmas 1918 there, as munition factory guards. We came back in February 1919 and marched through London, all the barracks were full so we stayed at Romford. We did duty at the Tower of London, locking up the tower and the ceremony of the keys, I wouldn't have missed that for anything.

On 31 January 1919, Cis Oakes (brother to Bert) wrote to his parents explaining they were 'moving about from one place to another', but were now settled at Lommersum in Germany. 'It's only just a country village, in fact it's not so large as our town, we are on police duty,' Cis explained before adding, 'Dad I must thank you very much for the great trouble you have gone to in sending an application for my release from the Army immediately.' It seems that some servicemen could be demobilised early if they were able to provide evidence for guaranteed employment. Not surprisingly Cis waited anxiously, 'when my allotment of a place comes through as a "Slip Man" I shall be released, so the sooner it comes now the better'.

'Time is very precious in the Army,' wrote Cis, as every serviceman, regular, conscript and volunteer was 'waiting for Demobilization to come and then we shall be able to sit round the old home fire, in the family circle and tell you all our little experiences etc.'.

In April 1919, the first of the Shropshire Regiments was back in Shrewsbury and the mayor placed a notice in the newspaper requesting 'tradesmen to decorate the route from the station to The Square and to the barracks' to welcome home the 1st Battalion of the King's Shropshire Light Infantry. Gradually the other battalions returned home, together with the Shropshire natives who had served in other regiments and services, and, on 19 July 1919, a Peace Day Celebration was organised. Although aimed principally at the children,

Many communities held celebrations to mark the end of the war and this one in Clun involved a fancy dress parade. The ladies appear to be representing the Allies: Japan, Russia, the United States of America, the United Kingdom, France, Serbia and Belgium (kneeling). (Kindly loaned by Ray Farlow)

many others joined in the festivities and it was estimated that over 6,000 children were given tea in the various schools and afterwards attended sports and games organised in Shrewsbury Quarry. Unfortunately, reported the newspaper, it rained heavily, but the streets remained crowded and many children were given joyrides around the town in one of the numerous motor vehicles that had gathered. On Tuesday, 5 August the Shropshire Peace Day and Victory March took place, a huge event that encompassed both the town of Shrewsbury and the Quarry.

Every community throughout Shropshire held peace celebrations in some form or another to welcome home those who had served in the war. In Ketley, a community east of Wellington, there was a procession through the parish composed of decorated vehicles and groups in fancy-dress costume. Tea was provided for the children and a meat tea for the demobilised men was followed by a sports competition; all the arrangements were admirably carried out by the committee. In Ash, near Whitchurch in north Shropshire, the eighty-two returning soldiers were welcomed home and each man received a silver-topped ash stick inscribed with his name and rank. Then, together with their relatives, they were treated to a substantial tea. Sadly eighteen men did not return to Ash and sympathy was extended to their families.

Sometimes individuals were recognised, Corporal Thomas Ellis of the 7th Battalion KSLI (who had been awarded the Military Medal in 1918), was presented with £100 by his employers at the Castle Works in Hadley. Sergeant Benjamin Peake, a choirmaster and member of Tan Bank Methodist church who had received the Distinguished Conduct Medal (DCM) for 'consistent good work with a section of machine guns', was also a Castle Works employee and was awarded twenty-five War Savings Stamps.

Many thousands of those returning home were wounded and suffering some physical disability. Winnie MacLeod remembered that her father, a member of the Royal Army Medical Corps, was invalided home. He was in hospital in Aldershot and the War Office offered money to enable her mother to visit him there. He remained in the army and became an aide-de-camp to a doctor at Sutton Coldfield.

William Lloyd had joined up in 1916 and was drafted into the Monmouth Regiment. During training he was injured in an accident and became concerned that he would have to return home. The medical board, discovering that he was a cobbler by trade, instead sent him to Belton Park Camp to repair the shoes of soldiers and officers. Once there, William was kept very busy, especially when it was discovered that he was able to make and repair shoes by hand: 'I did all the officers shoes, because I was a hand-sewn man.'

Other servicemen were medically discharged and most had to supplement their pension. Mr Samuel Jones from Hadley, for example, was left doubled up and paralysed from the effects of mustard gas poisoning. The local relief fund gave him £56 in order to buy a governess cart and a pony together with some poultry, thus enabling him to sell fruit, vegetables and eggs from the cart.

SHROPSHIRE PEACE DAY AND VICTORY MARCH

Shropshire gave its soldiers a warm welcome home on Tuesday, 5 August 1919 with around 6,000 troops marching from the racecourse at Monkmoor to Shrewsbury Quarry. Representatives of the nursing services also joined the soldiers in the parade through the town, 'It was a day of triumphs' said the newspaper, 'which the women deservedly shared just as much as the men.'

The mayor requested all businesses to close and a general holiday was observed; the streets were lined with bunting and welcome home banners were displayed all along the route. Floral arrangements under the direction of the park's supervisor, Mr Ward, decorated the Quarry and its entrance gates.

At noon the march began, led by the bands of the 2nd Battalion Cheshire Regiment and the 2nd Battalion South Wales Borderers. All along the route there were cheering crowds and the bells of both St Chads and St Mary's 'rang joyous peals'. From about 1.30 p.m. the Quarry hosted a Grand Athletic Carnival programme 'open to all men who have served in any branch of H.M. Forces who are natives of the county of Salop, or who are now resident in the county or men who have served in any of the Shropshire Regiments'.

Events included a regimental relay race, a six-a-side football competition and a tug of war; the Shropshire County Police 'A' Team beat the Shrewsbury Borough Police 'A' Team in a gripping tug-of-war final. Local bands played and musical entertainments in a large marquee attracted crowded audiences. There was a Grand Military Tattoo in the evening, while bands played in the streets and dancing continued until midnight. The *Shrewsbury Chronicle* reported that around 65,000 people watched the pageant with 'a striking absence of intemperance and disorder'.

County of Salop and Borough of Shrewsbury.

—

Celebration of Peace

❦❦

Official Programme

AND

Souvenir

OF

WELCOME HOME

to County and Borough, of Men of
Shropshire and Shropshire Units,
who have served Overseas.

AT

SHREWSBURY,

ON

TUESDAY, 5th AUGUST, 1919.

❦❦

GOD SAVE THE KING.

FLOREAT SALOPIA.

—

Price 6d.

*Peace Day and Victory March,
5 August 1919, the official
programme. (Shropshire Archives)*

*The stone cross memorial
located in front of the library
in Castle Street, Shrewsbury,
decorated for the Peace Day and
Victory March celebrations on
5 August 1919. (Kindly loaned by
Brian Curran)*

Guardsman Edward Ted Hough is seated on the left in a light-coloured shirt with a group of Grenadier Guardsmen. This could well be a training camp and dates from between November 1915, when Ted enlisted, and his injury in November 1916. (Author's collection)

Private 24401 Edward Hough, originally from Broseley, had joined the Grenadier Guards in November 1915 aged just 19 years. After training, he arrived in France in August 1916 where he received gunshot wounds in his right hand, resulting in the amputation of his forearm. Private Hough was discharged on 27 June 1917 as being 'no longer physically fit for war service' and was given a conditional pension of 27s 6d per week for nine weeks and then 16s 6d per week for life.

Before the war, Edward Hough had been a carpenter who, having had to leave school early following the death of his father, worked hard to educate himself. It is difficult to appreciate how he had to teach himself to write, adapt his carpentry and find employment on being left with this disability in order to keep his family. Like many others who had taken part in the war, he never spoke about the conditions or his experiences, instead he kept his thoughts and feelings very much to himself.

However, the Guards training never left him and he was always upright, smart and with well-polished shoes.

There were, of course, very many families who would never be the same again and whose husbands, fathers and sons (and, in a number of cases, mothers, wives and daughters) would not be coming home. Groups of friends headed out to war together from which not all of them returned. The following image, taken outside the Bulls Head, West Street, St Georges, in 1914, includes a group of six soldiers heading overseas, four of which would not survive the war. They have no known graves and are remembered on the memorials to the missing: Private Percy Tonks (age 23) of the 6th Battalion KSLI, died on 31 August 1916 and is commemorated on the Thiepval Memorial; Lance Corporal Aaron Hicks, (age 27) died 16 August 1917 and Lance Corporal Albert Benjamin Rushton (Sam) both of the 6th Battalion KSLI, died 19 September 1917; Private Bert Ryder (age 23) 1st/4th Battalion KSLI, died on 11 April 1918 and these last three are commemorated on the Tyne Cot Memorial.

From the very start of the conflict the local newspapers did not hesitate to record those who had died, very often including

Going off to war – from left to right: Percy Tonks, Aaron Hicks, Sam Rushton, Sidney Stevens, Polly Hicks, Jim Hicks, Bert Ryder, Mr Pessal and Maud Hicks. Sadly only two of these pals survived the war and Polly Hicks has her hands on their shoulders: Sidney Stevens and Jim Hicks. (Kindly loaned by Jim Cooper)

a photograph and biographical details of the serviceman. Commanding officers at the front sent letters of condolence to the grieving families: 'He was a good soldier and well liked … we feel his loss very much,' wrote the Company Sergeant on the death of Private Harold Hurdley of Broseley.

Some of these letters were very detailed, Captain F. Johnson, KSLI, writing to the widow of Private F. Boylin in April 1916, wrote that:

> … your husband was killed by a shell while in the trenches. His loss is very deeply regretted by the officers and men of his company, with whom he was very popular. He has been with me ever since the formation of the battalion in September 1914 and I am more than sorry to lose him.

Right from the beginning of the war there seems to have been no censorship on the reporting of casualties and the local Shropshire newspapers, especially the *Wellington Journal and Shrewsbury News*, published reports of those killed or wounded as well as details of missing servicemen and those taken as prisoners of war. At the end of each year a 'gallery' of photographs of 'gallant heroes who had made the final sacrifice' in the previous year was also published.

A number of popular literary figures, notably Sir Arthur Conan Doyle and Rudyard Kipling, had supported the war, attending recruiting rallies and writing propagandist material. Rupert Brooke, a young poet who served with the Royal Naval Division, also believed the war to be a just cause and wrote typically patriotic poems. What, for many young men, had started out in 1914 as a 'great adventure that would be over by Christmas', turned into a horrific stalemate particularly on the Western Front. Artists and writers began to produce more realistic illustrations of the conflict, Siegfried Sassoon, a decorated war hero, was sent to hospital where he met and encouraged another wounded officer and poet: Wilfred Owen.

Wilfred Edward Salter Owen

One of the most significant poets of the war, Wilfred Owen was born on 18 March 1893 in Oswestry and was educated for a short period at Shrewsbury before moving to France where he taught at the Berlitz School of English. He returned home during September 1915 and signed up to the Artists' Rifles, something he would not have be able to do earlier, being only 5ft 5in tall and so under the required height in 1914.

After training in London, Wilfred received his commission in the 5th Battalion Manchester Regiment and finally went to France in December 1916 where he proved himself to be an excellent shot. In May he was hit by a shell explosion which also killed his best friend and, when he was rescued, it was recognised that he was suffering from shell shock.

Wilfred was sent to Craiglockhart War Hospital in Edinburgh where he was encouraged by his doctor and Siegfried Sassoon to continue writing poetry. By the end of August 1918, Wilfred had rejoined his regiment and returned to the front; he would be awarded the Military Cross 'for conspicuous gallantry

The Wilfred Owen sculpture, Symmetry, by Paul de Monchaux. (Author's collection)

and devotion to duty on 1st/2nd October' whilst in action near Amiens.

2nd Lieutenant Wilfred Owen was shot and killed on 4 November 1918, just days before the Armistice, and is buried in the cemetery at Ors. It is said that his parents received notice of his death on Armistice Day as the church bells of Shrewsbury rang in celebration.

A sculpture in memory of Wilfred Owen was created by Paul de Monchaux and unveiled in June 1993. Named *Symmetry*, it was commissioned by the Wilfred Owen Association to commemorate the life and work of the poet and is sited in the grounds of Shrewsbury Abbey. The design is said to 'echo the symmetries of [the] poems, as well as the trenches of 1917 and the Sambrie-Oise Canal'. The line 'I am the enemy you killed, my friend', inscribed along one side, is from the poem 'Strange Meeting'.

Shot at Dawn

Shell shock was a condition that had initially not been acknowledged by the military medical staff, but as the war progressed it did become a recognised disorder. It seems probable that those who were able to, paid for continuing treatment when the sufferer came home, whilst those less able to pay, depending on the severity of the condition, were returned to their families and communities. Arthur Bland remembered a young man from Dawley who was known to have suffered shell shock, 'sometimes he was normal and sometimes he would be funny. Mother used to dread him coming into our house. Sometimes he would strip off and dance around.' It seems that generally these men were accepted back into a society that was aware of their condition – some of the young men who were in battle on the front line were not so lucky.

During the First World War the British and Commonwealth military command executed 306 of its own men for cowardice in the line of duty. Many of them were just boys, unable to cope with the scale of the destruction, carnage and death that they were living with every day; a few were driven insane but several just ran away. Once caught, a court martial followed and the sentence of execution generally took place the next day at dawn when the soldier, having sometimes been plied with alcohol (usually rum) throughout the night, was taken out, blindfolded and tied to a stake. The medical officer would then pin a piece of white cloth over the condemned man's heart and, on a given signal, the British Army firing squad would aim and fire. The firing squad usually consisted of six soldiers, sometimes from the accused's own regiment, and routinely there would be one blank round so that no soldier could be sure who had fired the fatal shot. Some soldiers, unsurprisingly, found being in the firing line-up traumatic so not all executions went smoothly. Immediately after the shots were taken the medical officer would examine the condemned man and, if he was still alive, the officer in charge would have to shoot him in the head with his revolver.

Private 40435 Denis Jetson Blakemore of the 8th Battalion North Staffordshire Regiment, was born in Bicton, Shrewsbury to George and Sophia, where his father was the local schoolmaster. Following his enlistment, Denis had served in Ireland before arriving in France in 1916. The following year, in May 1917, he was charged with desertion and, having been found guilty of absence without leave, was given fifteen years' penal servitude, suspended. He was sent back to his unit but, on 7 June 1917 at 5.40 a.m. and whilst waiting to go into attack, he was reported missing and was discovered hiding in a shell hole at the rear of the assembly trenches. Denis was sent to join up with his unit once more but went missing again.

1918 ELECTION RESULTS FOR SHROPSHIRE

William Bridgeman, Coalition Conservative was returned for Oswestry with a majority of 3,809. He had served as the parliamentary secretary to the Minister of Labour from 1916–19.

George Butler Lloyd, Coalition Conservative was returned for Shrewsbury with a majority of 4,328.

Sir Charles S. Henry, Coalition Liberal was returned unopposed for the Wrekin.

Captain Sir Breville Stanier, unionist was returned unopposed for Ludlow.

At his court martial he pleaded not guilty saying, 'I was too upset to go on with my own section; I knew the attack was coming off that morning.' There was no reprieve, however, and Private Denis Blakemore was found guilty of desertion and sentenced to death. The sentence was carried out at 4.30 a.m. on 9 July 1917 and he was buried in Belgium in the Locre Hospice Cemetery.

Generally these soldiers were not included on their local war memorials. This, however, was not the case with Private Blakemore; his name is clearly on the plaque in St Georges church, Frankwell, Shrewsbury and was apparently inscribed there from the outset.

Repatriation of British-held Prisoners of War

As well as the repatriation of British prisoners of war, the German prisoners also needed to be sent home. In some cases, however, there appeared to be a delay in completing this operation. At the Park Hall prisoner-of-war camp near Oswestry, this led to some unruly behaviour, with difficulties commencing when German officers encouraged their fellow prisoners to refuse to parade for roll call. Tensions continued to increase, resulting in several hundred prisoners gathering at the sentry's guard house where they began to throw stones and shout. Private Maycock, believing that a prison riot threatened, gave a warning that if they did not disperse he would fire and then, when the disturbances continues, he fired a warning shot towards the latrines. Unfortunately, at that moment, 20-year-old Willie Oster had decided to climb the latrine and was shot and killed; an inquest returned a verdict of misadventure. Willie Oster was initially buried, with full military honours, in Park Hall German Cemetery, but later his remains were reinterred in the German Military Cemetery on Cannock Chase.

Amongst the German officers was Admiral Von Reuter, who had commanded the Imperial German Navy's High Seas Fleet when it was interned at Scapa Flow. In order to prevent the British seizing the ships, the admiral had ordered the scuttling of the fleet on 21 June 1919. Following this incident Von Reuter, together with the remaining crews, were taken as prisoners of war and eventually interned at the Park Hall Camp Oswestry.

Although hostilities were over, the Germans were still held at the camp. However, it appears the officers were allowed out into Oswestry and it was whilst Admiral Von Reuter was being conducted to a local bank that he was recognised and mobbed. The crowd jostled and jeered the men and someone threw a rotten egg which hit the admiral on the cheek before he was escorted away in his car. Eventually Von Reuter was moved to Donington Hall, near Shrewsbury in a 'closed motorcar' together with the commandant of the German Officers' Internment Camp and his servants, whilst the rest of the staff remained at Oswestry. Admiral Von Reuter and the remaining prisoners from Oswestry were finally repatriated in January 1920.

'Spanish' Influenza Pandemic

During 1918 and into 1919, an influenza pandemic swept around the world: current estimates state that between 50 million and 100 million people were killed by the virus 'in every corner of the globe'. Although war was not the cause of the influenza, it is certain that the circumstances of the war accelerated the spread, especially when infected soldiers were sent back from the front in crowded trains to equally crowded casualty clearing stations and hospitals which often had a shortage of doctors.

The virus became known as 'Spanish flu' not because it originated in Spain but because, as a neutral country, Spain had no restrictions on publishing. In Britain, despite the pressure to censor, local newspapers did print reports but they were usually short and tucked away

> **SPANISH FLU**
> A schoolgirl later recalled: 'There were many deaths in Madeley, my father being one of them. I caught it from him but lived to tell the tale. Death was not a stranger in many homes due to the terrible casualties in the war.'

NO PINEAPPLES!

The casualties of the conflict were not just the maimed and disabled. Soldier suffered the effects of their experiences in many forms: 'After the war pineapple was never served in Grandma's house because Uncle had been gassed and could not stand the smell of it' recalled one local who, as a child, had been told that the tinned fruit was banned at their grandparents' house for this reason.

amid other local news. The *Western Times* stated on 5 July 1918 that a school in Devon was closed as '100 children and 2 teachers had been absent for some days', although the Shropshire newspapers made little reference until October 1918 when they reported that: 'IRONBRIDGE – the epidemic is spreading in the district, several deaths have occurred. All the day schools are closed, also at Broseley, Madeley and Coalbrookdale as a result of the malady.'

In Coalport it was recorded that five deaths had occurred and fifty people were absent from the Coalport China Works due to the influenza. A sad case concerned a Private Charley Sherwood of Woodhouse Lane, Horsehay who was home on leave from Italy. He had served both in France and Italy and whilst at home he was taken ill and died some three or four days after his arrival. He was 32 years old and had a wife and two children.

A number of deaths were recorded in Hadley: Mrs Edith Dobell, whose husband was in Egypt, left 'two little children' and it was noted that 'the schools were still closed and in nearly every home one or two are down with the malady'.

1918 General Election

By December 1918 'influenza news' was replaced by information regarding the forthcoming general election; this would be the first election in which all men over the age of 21 and all women over the age of 30 would be able to exercise their right to vote. The polling was held on Saturday, 14 December 1918 but the counting did not take place until 28 December in order to transport the votes from soldiers serving overseas.

In Shropshire there had been boundary changes which had created four new constituencies but, considering this was the first time many had voted in a general election, the turnout was poor. This coincided with national figures, which also reported a poor turnout with just over 50 per cent of those able to vote actually doing so. In the end the coalition won a landslide victory, with Mr Lloyd George remaining as prime minister.

Postscript

Legacy

In his 1918 manifesto, David Lloyd George campaigned for a 'land fit for heroes' but, with a national debt that had increased about twelvefold during the war, financial support for any schemes would be difficult. The traditional heavy industries, following the economic boom of war production, began to find competition difficult with the loss of foreign markets and a lack of pre-war investment. As a result unemployment increased, reaching its highest levels in 1921. In Shropshire the industrial landscape of the coalfield was grim: the Lilleshall Company began to reduce and close a number of its departments; the less viable collieries closed; and, following a takeover in 1926, the Coalport China Works closed, moving all its operations to Stoke.

Most major sectors of agriculture followed a similar pattern and increased taxation was one of the reasons that forced many of the great estates to be sold, either completely or piecemeal. One of the most significant changes in post-war rural Shropshire was the final sale of the huge Lilleshall Estate, owned by the Duke of Sutherland, while other similar sales often severed a family connection to Shropshire that had been maintained for hundreds of years. As a result, many tenants took the opportunity to purchase their property and, whilst the number of owner-occupied farms increased within the county, the actual size of landholding decreased while the expansion in the use of tractors and other farm machinery reduced the need for as many labourers.

The economic cost of the conflict was great but not as devastating as the terrible loss of life; it has been estimated that, overall, in excess of 10 million people died in the Great War. Over 750,000 were from Britain, with a further 200,000 from the Empire, including nearly a third from the Indian subcontinent. In addition to those who died directly from battle, there were those who suffered the effects of gas, or shell shock and, in the Middle East particularly, from malaria and fever.

It would be almost impossible to calculate the number of casualties among Shropshire's soldiers. The King's Shropshire Light Infantry published a list of well over 4,000 of their men who died between 1914 and 1919 and whilst this list includes men from outside the county who served in the 'Shropshires', it does not, of course, cover those Shropshire men who served in other regiments and services, in the Royal Navy, in the Royal Flying Corps or those who died of their injuries at a later date. Neither does it count the women of the county who served in a variety of capacities at the battlefields as well as at home. Many served as nursing staff, but women were also both ambulance and car drivers and employed in administration and catering departments.

By direction of His Grace the Duke of Sutherland.

SHROPSHIRE.

Illustrated Particulars with Plans and Conditions of Sale of the very Valuable

Freehold, Residential, Agricultural, Sporting, Licensed & Cottage Properties,

the whole forming

The Lilleshall Estate,

Situate in the Parishes of Lilleshall, Sheriffhales, Chetwynd Aston, Shifnal and Kinnersley.

To be Sold by Auction

IN 268 LOTS

By Messrs. BARBER & SON, Wellington, Salop; and Messrs. KNIGHT, FRANK & RUTLEY, Hanover Square, London.

Lots 1 and 2
To be offered in The Sale Rooms of Messrs. KNIGHT, FRANK & RUTLEY, at 20, Hanover Square, London, on Monday, the 23rd July, 1917, at 2.30 p.m. precisely.

Lots 3 to 268 inclusive
To be offered at the Town Hall, Wellington, on Tuesday, Wednesday, Thursday & Friday, July 24th, 25th, 26th and 27th, 1917. Commencing at Two o'clock prompt each day.

Further Information and Cards to view from the Auctioneers.

SOLICITORS	LAND AGENT
Messrs. R. S. TAYLOR, SON & HUMBERT 4, FIELD COURT, GRAY'S INN LONDON, W.C. 1 Telephone No. 16, Holborn	F. TODD, ESQ. TRENTHAM ESTATE OFFICE STOKE-ON-TRENT Telephone, No. 11, Trentham

AUCTIONEERS

Messrs. KNIGHT, FRANK & RUTLEY 20, HANOVER SQUARE LONDON, W. 1 & EDINBURGH. Telephone No. 1942, Gerrard (4 lines)	Messrs. BARBER & SON CHURCH STREET WELLINGTON, SALOP Telephone No. 27, Wellington

The front page of the Lilleshall Estate sale of 1917. (Ironbridge Gorge Museum Trust)

Commonwealth War Graves

Sir Fabian Ware, a commander of a mobile Red Cross unit in France, became increasingly concerned about the graves of men killed during the conflict, and under his instruction the unit began recording and caring for all graves they could find. Eventually this work was given official recognition by the War Office and, in May 1917, the Imperial War Graves Commission (later the Commonwealth War Graves Commission) was established by Royal Charter. Soon after the Armistice their work began in earnest until, by the end of 1918, 587,000 graves had been identified and a further 559,000 soldiers were registered as having no known grave.

The mandate of the commission was that the bodies would not be repatriated and that any memorial should be uniform, avoiding any class distinction. Ware asked eminent architects of the day, including Sir Edward Lutyens, to oversee the design of cemeteries and memorials, whilst Rudyard Kipling was to advise on the inscriptions. The white headstone of Portland stone is now recognisable in illustrations of the many military cemeteries, particularly those in France and Belgium where they stand in row after row. The commemoration of those whose bodies were never found led to the construction of monuments, the largest and most impressive of which is the Thiepval Memorial Arch on which is inscribed 73,357 names of those missing from the Somme offensive of 1916.

In Shropshire there are over 700 Commonwealth War Graves sited in some 148 cemeteries and churchyards throughout the county. The youngest was Henry G. Price, 2nd Class J/31453 Royal Navy, who served aboard HMS *Impregnable*; he died on 29 December 1914, aged just 16, and is buried in Meole Brace. The oldest was Private 18636 William Clewett of the Royal Defence Corps, who died on 6 May 1920 aged 60; he was the husband of Eliza and lived at Butcher Row in Shrewsbury. There are also three women, two who served in Queen Mary's Army Auxiliary Corps (QMAAC), and a nurse from Queen Alexandra's Imperial Military Nursing Service (QAIMNS).

Queen Mary's Army Auxiliary Corps was originally formed as the Women's Auxiliary Army Corps in 1917 and was renamed in 1918; its members staffed the restaurants, canteens and refreshment facilities for the armed services both at home and overseas. On 31 March 1917 the first fourteen cooks and waitress were sent to the battlefields and in total over 57,000 women served between January 1917 and November 1918. Assistant Waitress 21513 Edith Esther Pickering is the youngest woman buried in a Commonwealth War Grave in Shropshire. Edith had been stationed on the Isle of Wight for a short period and had also been in Portsmouth. She was home on leave when she was taken ill and died within the week, on 2 October 1919, aged only 19. Another local woman, Hilda Jones (classed as Worker 40840 with the QMAAC), died on 1 May 1920 and was buried in St Michael's churchyard, Welshampton. She had been working at the hostel near Borstal Heath and was the daughter of David and Mary Jones, who had also lost their son, William, a Private in the KSLI; he had died aged 21 on 18 October 1917 of wounds received in action.

Commonwealth War Grave of Miss Edith Esther Pickering, daughter of William and Mary Pickering of No. 73 Old Park, Dawley, in Malinslee churchyard. (Author's collection)

The Queen Alexandra's Imperial Military Nursing Service was established by Royal Warrant in 1902 and replaced the Army Nursing Service. Staff Nurse 2/Res/T66 Eugenie Elizabeth Teggin of the QAIMNS was the daughter of John and Mary Teggin of The Willows, St Martin Moors; she died on 25 December 1918, aged 28 and is buried in St Martin's of Tours churchyard, St Martins. Eugenie did her training at the General Infirmary in Dewsbury, having been a probationer nurse at the Queen Victoria Memorial Institution in Welshpool for two years. In April 1916 she left Dewsbury and began working at the New Zealand Military Hospital in Walton-on-Thames. From there Eugenie applied to join the QAIMNS for the duration of the war. On being accepted she was sent to Salonika where she arrived in October 1916 and stayed throughout the war. In December 1918 she was granted home leave and tragically contracted influenza and died whilst at home in Oswestry.

There was probably not a home in the county which remained untouched by the war; where a family member had not returned or had been disabled in one form or another and whose suffering was a constant reminder of the conflict. During the war some communities, as news of casualties reached home, began recording their own Roll of Honour and almost as soon as the Armistice had been declared, local committees began to be organised in order to discuss how to honour and remember those who had died.

Shropshire Memorials

Many parishes, towns and villages felt the need to create some form of permanent recognition for those who had given their lives. Similarly, local companies and businesses, railway stations and post offices all produced their own memorials in order to acknowledge their former employees. There was, however, no overall national movement or central guidance orchestrated by the government to acknowledge the fallen. In general a committee of local people, usually organised by the vicar, was set up to raise funds in order that a memorial could be established.

In Ketley, for example, the committee divided the parish into eight sections and the collectors were to 'call periodically so that the donation' could be spread over six months. Broseley War Memorial Fund published its accounts and showed that the largest contribution came from individual donations, with gifts from £25 to 6d (or whatever people were able to afford) which was added to that collected from fund-raising concerts and events.

A panel on the memorial park gates in Oakengates shows the name of N. Twigger. Private Noah Twigger, of No. 37 Station Road, Oakengates had served nine years with the KSLI in India and whilst a reservist he had been employed as a miner at the Freehold Pits. He rejoined at the outbreak of the war and, at great risk to his own life, rescued a wounded man of the West Yorkshire Regiment, bringing him back to the British

TO THE GLORY OF GOD

AND IN
HONOUR OF THE FALLEN
GREAT WAR 1914-1918.

HOLLINGSWORTH F.	PTE	R.W.F.
JONES J. E.	PTE	K.S.L.I.
KNAPTON L.S.	PTE	2ND DORSETS.
KNOWLES S.	PTE	K.S.L.I.
LLOYD A.	PTE	K.S.L.I.
MANSELL W.W.	PTE	K.S.L.I.
MAWDSLEY H.	PTE	K.S.L.I.
MEESON C.W.	PTE	R.A.M.C.
MERRINGTON A.P.	CPL	ARTISTS RIFLES.
MERRINGTON H.W.	CPL	1ST HEREFORDS.
PLANT C.	GNR	R.G.A.
PLANT J.E.	PTE	K.S.L.I.
PLANT S.	PTE	KINGS LIVERPOOL.
PLANT T.	SAPPER	R.E.
PODMORE G.	PTE	K.S.L.I.
RICHARDS H.	PTE	15TH CHESHIRES.
SABBEN J.C.F.	PTE	YORKS & LANCS.
SAMUELS F.	PTE	K.S.L.I.
SHENTON E.	PTE	K.S.L.I.
SHENTON W.	PTE	K.S.L.I.
SMALL E.	PTE	R. WARWICKS.
TAYLOR G.	CPL	K.S.L.I.
THORBURN J.A.	L/SGT	R. WARWICKS.
TRANTER W.H.	PTE	K.S.L.I.
TREVOR A.	PTE	K.S.L.I.
TWIGGER N.	L/CPL	K.S.L.I.
WITHINGTON J.W.	PTE	20TH MANCHESTERS.

Memorial park gates in Oakengates where Private Noah Twigger is commemorated. Despite a local newspaper reporting that his 'gallantry is to be recognised by conferring the Distinguished Conduct Medal upon him, a distinction which he will have thoroughly earned' it seems he never was awarded the DCM, but by the time of his death had been promoted to lance corporal. (Author's collection)

trenches and miraculously escaping 'a shower of German bullets'. He was granted a few days' home leave in recognition of this act of bravery and, as he left to return to the trenches, the Boys' Life Brigade marched up to cheer him off. Private Twigger was reported wounded and missing on 9 August 1915. His body was never found and he is remembered on the Menin Gate memorial at Ypres.

Local memorials, such as the park gates in Oakengates, took on many different forms, from a classical cenotaph or figure of a soldier to village halls and community spaces. One of the more unusual memorials was the Coalport and Jackfield Footbridge which was built by public subscription for about £1,200. The bridge was opened on 22 September 1922 by Lord and Lady Forester of Willey Hall and replaced a ferry boat which had 'served its purpose for 120 years'. As the ribbon was cut, Lady Forester wished the bridge 'a long and happy life'.

A Remembrance Day was designated in 1919 on the first anniversary of the signing of the Armistice: the eleventh hour of the eleventh day of the eleventh month. The *Manchester Guardian* reported the 'The First Two Minute Silence in London':

The first stroke of eleven produced a magical effect. The tram cars glided into stillness, motors ceased to cough and fume, and stopped dead, and the mighty-limbed dray horses hunched back upon their loads and stopped also, seeming to do it of their own volition.

Someone took off his hat, and with a nervous hesitancy the rest of the men bowed their heads also. Here and there an old soldier could be detected slipping unconsciously into the posture of 'attention'. An elderly woman, not far away, wiped her eyes, and the man beside her looked white and stern. Everyone stood very still … The hush deepened. It had spread over the whole city and become so pronounced as to impress one with a sense of audibility. It was a silence which was almost pain … And the spirit of memory brooded over it all.

Local memorials became the focus for Remembrance Day as around the country communities adopted a similar format of parades and services and, at 11.00 a.m., two minutes' silence. This is continued today and includes all servicemen and women killed in conflicts since the First World War, although the commemorations now generally take place on the nearest Sunday.

The red poppy is the emblem that has come to represent Remembrance Day in Great Britain; inspired by the poem 'In Flanders Fields' by Major John McCrae, it was first adopted by the Royal British Legion in 1921. Paper poppies are now sold by volunteers in the lead up to Remembrance Day on behalf of the Royal British Legion and wreaths of these poppies are laid at war memorials by services, clubs and institutions.

The money raised through the 'Poppy Appeal' is used to help servicemen and women from all three services, with a substantial amount supporting the Battle Back Centre. This is a sports and adventure activities centre established at Lilleshall Hall, the former home of the Dukes of Sutherland, for wounded and injured service personnel.

The opening of the Coalport and Jackfield Memorial Bridge on 22 September 1922. A plaque on the bridge names the twenty-six men from the area who died in the First World War and eight from the Second World War. (Ironbridge Gorge Museum Trust)

Thankful Villages

The term 'Thankful Villages' was popularised during the 1930s by writer Arthur Mee and stood for those communities whose men all returned home from the war. There are fifty-two villages in England and Wales now recognised, with thirteen being 'Doubly Thankful', having had all their service personnel also return from the Second World War. In Shropshire, the village of Harley situated at the foot of Wenlock Edge, is a thankful village that saw all twenty of its men return home.

But a generation had virtually been lost. A young Shropshire woman remembered that all the girls were 'deprived of food, new clothes, proper shoes, boyfriends, parties and kisses' and that after the war, with little prospect of marriage or family, they went to work, joining the civil service, or colleges and teaching hospitals, and became 'dedicated spinsters who held the schools and hospitals together'.

British society had begun to change, even down to the spoken word. Arthur Lewis from Madeley noticed the returning men had begun to lose the local dialect: 'chaps who had been away at the war [were] coming back saying you instead of thee.'

BIBLIOGRAPHY

Books

County Recruiting Aid Committee Minutes

Gale, W.K.V. & Nicholls, C.R., *The Lilleshall Company, a History 1764–1964* (Moorland Publishing Co. Ltd, 1979)

Neal, Toby, *Owd Jockeys at War – The Remarkable Story of the Dawley News*, Vol. 1: 1915–16 (Langrish Caiger Publications, 2004)

Rowley, Trevor, *The Shropshire Landscape* (Hodder & Stoughton, 1972)

Trinder, Barrie, *The History of Shropshire* (Phillimore, 1983)

Vale, Edmund, *Shropshire* (Robert Hale Ltd., 1949)

Williams, Dr Heather, *The Lure of the Land – A Century of Education at Harper Adams College* (Harper Adams Agricultural College, 2000)

Newspapers

Shrewsbury Chronicle

Wellington Journal and Shrewbury News

Great War Britain:
The First World War at Home

LUCI GOSLING

After the declaration of war in 1914, the conflict dominated civilian life for the next four years. Magazines quickly adapted without losing their gossipy essence: fashion jostled for position with items on patriotic fund-raising, and court presentations were replaced by notes on nursing. The result is a fascinating, amusing and uniquely feminine perspective of life on the home front.

978 0 7524 9188 2

The Workers' War:
British Industry and the First World War

ANTHONY BURTON

The First World War didn't just rock the nation in terms of bloodshed: it was a war of technological and industrial advances. Working Britain experienced change as well: with the men at war, it fell to the women of the country to keep the factories going. Anthony Burton explores that change.

978 0 7524 9886 7